# BEYOND SLAVERY

## AFRICAN AMERICANS FROM EMANCIPATION TO TODAY

# BEYOND SLAVERY

## AFRICAN AMERICANS FROM EMANCIPATION TO TODAY

Ann Byers

**Enslow Publishing**
101 W. 23rd Street
Suite 240
New York, NY 10011
USA
enslow.com

Published in 2017 by Enslow Publishing, LLC
101 W. 23rd Street, Suite 240, New York, NY 10011

**Library of Congress Cataloging-in-Publication Data**

Names: Byers, Ann, author.
Title: Beyond slavery : African Americans from emancipation to today / Ann Byers.
Description: New York, NY : Enslow Publishing, 2017. | Series: Slavery and slave resistance | Includes
bibliographical references and index. |
 Audience: Grade 9 to 12.
Identifiers: LCCN 2016004683 | ISBN 9780766075474 (library bound)
Subjects: LCSH: African Americans—History—20th century. | African Americans—History—19th
century. | Civil rights movements--United States--History--20th century. | Civil rights movements-
-United States—History—19th century. | United States—Race relations.
Classification: LCC E185.6 .B95 2016 | DDC 323.1196/0730904—dc23
LC record available at http://lccn.loc.gov/2016004683

Printed in the United States of America

**To Our Readers:** We have done our best to make sure all website addresses in this book were active
and appropriate when we went to press. However, the author and the publisher have no control over
and assume no liability for the material available on those websites or on any websites they may link
to. Any comments or suggestions can be sent by e-mail to customerservice@enslow.com.

Portions of this book appeared in the book *African-American History From Emancipation to Today:
Rising Above the Ashes of Slavery.*

# CONTENTS

# INTRODUCTION

Everyone heard it clearly; it was the horn. But why was it sounding now, in the middle of the day? The horn was the signal to start or stop work, and it was much too early to stop. In the morning, when the slaves on this Arkansas plantation heard the horn, they marched into the fields to begin their day's labor. Just before dark, its welcome blast called them back to their log houses. The horn never sounded in the middle of the day. Something was wrong.

The two hundred African-American men and women in the fields paused at their work. What could the sound mean? The overseer had left earlier that day, so there was no one to tell the slaves what to do. They decided it must have been a mistake. It was the wrong time, so they went back to chopping cotton.

The horn blared a second time. One of the workers yelled to the head slave, "We better go on it. Dat our horn."[1]

The head slave hesitated. He was afraid they would get in trouble if they quit without the overseer there.

Everyone was afraid of the white overseer, Mr. Saunders. Some of them had felt his whip draw blood on their bare backs. Most had witnessed him beat one slave to death and toss his body into a pond. All of them had heard him threaten that he would set free with his shotgun

6

anyone who missed "one toot of the horn." So, they argued about what to do. Finally, they lined up and headed in.

Mr. Saunders was sitting on the porch of his house with a man they had never seen. The stranger stood up and spoke directly to the slaves. "You . . . know what day dis is?" he asked. No one answered.

ATION OF THE ABOLITION OF SLAVERY IN THE DISTRICT OF COLUMBIA BY THE COLORED PEOPLE, IN WASHINGTON, APRIL 19, 1866.—[SKETCHED BY F. DIELMAN.]

Great numbers of African Americans in Washington, D.C., celebrated the end of slavery. The news came as a surprise to many slaves. What would happen, now that they were free?

"Well," the man said, "dis de fourth day of June, and dis is 1865. I want you all to 'member de date 'cause you [are always] going to remember de day. Today you is free. . . . you don't have to git up and go by de horn any more. You is your own bosses now." He also said the slaves were just the same as "all us white people."[2]

June 4, 1865, was almost two full months after the Civil War had ended and two and a half years after the Emancipation Proclamation had legally freed all slaves in Arkansas and other states in rebellion. On June 4, 1865, the news finally reached the Jones plantation. These slaves were really, truly free![3]

# SLAVERY AND THE ECONOMY OF THE SOUTH

Most African Americans had never experienced freedom. Many had been born into slavery, as had their ancestors before them. By 1865, slavery had been part of American culture for more than two hundred years. Africans had been brought to America's first colony, Jamestown, in 1619. By 1760, 250,000 African slaves toiled in the colonies, mainly in the South.[4]

When colonists settled the New World, they found that tobacco grew well in the rich soil of Maryland, Virginia, and North Carolina. And it sold well in England. But planting, growing, and harvesting tobacco required much work, and plantation owners knew they could profit most by using slaves.

Slave traders kidnapped men, women, and children in Africa. Sometimes they bought people from warring African chieftains who had captured them in battle. The traders brought them across the ocean in the dark holds of slave ships. They sold them to eager landowners in the Caribbean and North and South America. The demand for slave labor took a giant leap in the 1820s. By then, the invention of the cotton gin had made cotton a very profitable crop. At the same time, tobacco prices were dropping. Many tobacco farmers in Maryland and Virginia sold their lands and moved to the lower South to plant cotton. Throughout Alabama, Arkansas, Georgia, Mississippi, Louisiana, South Carolina, and Texas, cotton became the main crop.

Cotton made many Southern landowners rich. Production of cotton was so profitable that the South developed very little other industry. Its few manufacturing businesses and merchants were connected with the cotton trade. The Southern economy depended on cotton, and many white planters felt that cotton depended on slavery.

# SLAVERY AND SOCIETY IN THE SOUTH

Cotton shaped the economy of the South, and slavery helped shape Southern society. Although only one fourth of the white families in the southern states owned slaves, that minority tended to be wealthy and powerful.[5] Most had become rich only recently, and they wanted to create an image of themselves as lords and ladies. So, in addition to using slaves in their fields, they used them as cooks, butlers, coachmen, and nursemaids to their children. White Southerners enacted slave codes that prevented the slaves from rising above their low positions. Under these laws, a slave could not own property. Slaves could not gather with other slaves without a white person present. They could not be out after dark. Whites were forbidden to teach slaves to read and write. Slaves could not hit a white person even in self-defense, and slaves could rarely testify in court against a white person.

Even though the majority of whites in the South owned no slaves, most went along with slavery. They needed the plantation owners. The planters let them use their cotton gins, bought the produce from their small farms, and lent them money. For even the poorest of Southern whites, the institution of slavery raised them at least one rung on the social ladder. As long as the black man was on the bottom, the least fortunate white person had some social standing.

# STATUS OF SLAVES

The slave, of course, had no social status in the eyes of many whites. The slave had no money, no opportunity, and no rights. Slaves were thought of as property to be bought and sold. After a law was passed in 1808, no new slaves could be brought to America, but the slaves already in the country, as well as their children, could be bought and sold. Slave traders drove them to large auctions where landowners bid on them. The slaves were paraded in front of prospective buyers. Very often families were separated as mothers, fathers, and children were purchased by different masters.

As property, slaves were not citizens and therefore had no protection under the law. A master could beat and even kill his slave without fear of serious punishment. Many masters did not abuse their slaves physically, but many others were cruel to them.

Some slaves rebelled, but the uprisings were crushed mercilessly. Some tried to run away, but they were hunted with bloodhounds and killed or punished harshly if they were caught.

Even former slaves who had been granted freedom did not have the privileges or rights of citizens. They could not own land. They could not vote. Freed blacks had to show papers proving their freed status. Still, they were frequently arrested by slave traders as runaways and sold again on the auction block.

These are the abuses emancipation put to an end. Freedom did not even begin to solve all the problems or correct the injustices of two hundred years of slavery. But freedom was a first step in stopping the inhumane treatment. As one former slave said, "Slave days were bad, even if the master was what you call good. . . . But the freedom done away with all that whipping and beating."[6]

# CHAPTER 1

# REALLY FREE?

## 1865-1866

The Emancipation Proclamation Abraham Lincoln delivered in 1863 was directed to the Confederate states, the states of the South that had rebelled. The proclamation declared all slaves in those states to be free. But the document had no legal effect on any slave in states that had remained loyal to the United States. In order to ensure that all slaves in the entire country were really free, the Constitution had to be changed. So, after the war Congress added the Thirteenth Amendment to the Constitution. The amendment made very clear that slavery "shall not exist" anywhere in the United States. The Thirteenth Amendment became law in December 1865.

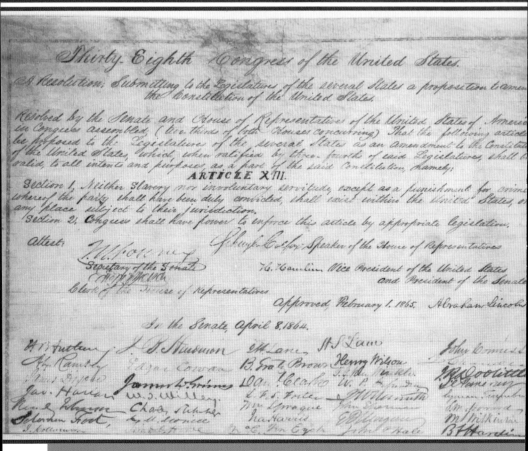

The Thirteenth Amendment formally abolished slavery in the United States. Its language plainly states, "Neither slavery nor involuntary servitude ... shall exist within the United States ..."

Freedom brought sudden and radical change to the South. The institution of slavery was now gone, and with it an unpaid labor force. Without slaves, how could the farms and farmers of the South continue to profit so greatly?

The 4 million freed slaves had even more troubling questions. Without their owners, how would they obtain housing, clothing, and food? How should they relate to their former owners? Were they really "just the same as" white people?

> I was free, and I didn't have nowhere to go. I didn't have nowhere to sleep. I didn't know what to do. My brother and I was together. ... After we got free we didn't know nothing to do. And my mother, she ... hunted places, and bound us out for a dollar a month, and we stay there maybe a couple of years. And, she'd come over and collect the money every month. And ... the men used to work for ten dollars a month, hundred and twenty dollars a year.[1]

# RACIST MINDSET

Most of the white people in the South could not imagine African Americans ever being "just the same as" they. Ever since 1619, when Africans were brought to Jamestown as workers, the white settlers considered themselves superior to the darker Africans. This was partially because of the great differences between the two cultures. The settlers were freedom-loving people. They needed to find a way to justify holding other human beings in bondage. Many colonists decided that God had created the two races different in nature. "The African has been, in all ages, a savage or a slave," wrote a former governor of South Carolina. "God created him inferior to the white man in form, color and intellect."[2]

Many came to believe that a black person was a little above animal. One Southerner claimed that the African "was brought to our shores a naked, brutish, unclean, captive, pagan savage, to be . . . a kind of connecting link between man and the beasts of burden."[3] Those who held this belief twisted science and the Bible to support their argument.

Many white slaveholders thought African Americans were able to perform only menial jobs—tasks that required little reasoning,

A DAY'S WORK ENDED.—Drawn by Matt Morgan.
See page 235.

Slaves were made to endure backbreaking work. WhItes justified this treatment by believing that the black race was intellectually inferior and built for physical labor.

knowledge, or skill. The people in power believed that the white race was made to rule and the black race was made to serve. "The supremacy of the white race . . . must be maintained forever," the editor of an Atlanta newspaper declared, ". . . because the white race is the superior race."[4]

Some Southerners, like the president of a North Carolina college, thought of African Americans as a "child race."[5] They believed that white landowners had an obligation to take care of blacks because blacks were not able to care for themselves.

At first, the concept of the black race as inferior, childlike, and fit only for menial labor was a way of justifying slavery. But over the course of six or more generations of slavery, these attitudes became set in the minds of many whites.

These attitudes were not limited to the South. Even though many people in the North were against slavery, they held some of the same prejudices as Southerners. The majority considered blacks—slave or free—inferior to whites. Less than a month after the Thirteenth Amendment was ratified, Pennsylvania representative Benjamin Boyer told Congress that African Americans belong to a "race by nature inferior" and are therefore "not the equals of white Americans."[6]

As soon as the Civil War began, some slaves escaped and fled to Union lines. This negated the common misconception by whites that slaves were happy to be living in servitude.

# BECOMING FREE

Although racial attitudes were unchanged, no longer could a white aristocracy command the obedience of blacks. African Americans might not be considered "just the same as" their former masters, but they would never be slaves again.

Before their emancipation, slaves were expected to do exactly what their owners told them to do. After emancipation, some slaves exercised their freedom by refusing to work. Some expressed their freedom by addressing their former owners disrespectfully. In a few places, some rose up in violence against cruel planters, but these incidents were not common.

During slavery, African-American families had been torn apart as members were sold to different plantations. Once they were free, some slaves went in search of their parents, spouses, and children. Others journeyed to the cities of the North and West, hoping to begin life new there.

Although many of the former slaves owned nothing, they found ways to leave their old masters' property. Many moved out of the slave quarters. Some lived instead in huts scattered around the old plantations. Others went to neighboring fields, deciding they would choose for whom they would work.

Few of the once-prosperous landowners of the South could afford to hire the former slaves. However, they devised a way to keep African Americans on their land as field workers without putting out any money: sharecropping.

# SHARING THE FIELDS AND THE PROFIT

Sharecropping was a simple concept: blacks would work the land that whites owned, and all would share in the harvest. The landowner contributed his land and seed; the workers contributed their labor. It seemed a fair arrangement. But in reality, the landowner benefited greatly and the worker barely got the necessities of life.

Sometime before the growing season began, the sharecropper went to the owner's house to make the arrangements. They negotiated how many acres of cotton and corn the sharecropper's family would plant, how much money the family would need for groceries, and what share of the crop the family would receive.

The landowner was not willing or able to pay his workers before the crop was harvested. So, he instructed the sharecropper to buy what he needed at a particular store. Sometimes the landowner also owned the store. Since the sharecropper did not have money, he had to

One option for former slaves upon emancipation was sharecropping. This involved the same kind of labor but under the guise of independence. The reality was far different.

While a slave, I was, as it were, groping in the dark, no ray of light penetrating the intense gloom surrounding me. My scanty garments felt too tight for me, my very respiration seemed to be restrained by some supernatural power. Now, free as I supposed, I felt like a bird on a pleasant May morning. Instead of the darkness of slavery, my eyes were almost blinded by the light of freedom.[7]

buy on credit. The storekeeper gave the worker what he needed—up to the agreed-upon amount—and charged the purchase to the owner.

The storekeeper would not receive his money until the crops came in, so he charged the sharecropper interest. The landowner also charged the sharecropper interest because he was "carrying the loan"—he was guaranteeing that it would be paid. The total interest was never less than 25 percent and was usually 40 to 80 percent. Sometimes it was as high as 200 percent.[8] The money—the original amount and interest—had to come out of the sharecropper's portion of the crops at harvest.

Even in a good year, the sharecropper usually owed more than the amount he received from his share of the crops. So, the sharecropper was in debt to the landowner. To work off the debt, the sharecropper had to stay with the planter through the next season. And in the next season, the cycle of borrowing, working, and owing would be repeated. For the majority of sharecroppers, however, life continued much as it had as under slavery.

But to former slaves, freedom meant independence. They would not be free until they could own land, send their children to school, and vote. As one newly freed black man put it, "If I cannot do like a white man, I am not free."[9]

# CHAPTER 2

# FREEDOM IS NOT EQUALITY: 1865–1877

The difficulties of the newly freed slaves did not come as a surprise to the U.S. government. As the Civil War was ending, President Abraham Lincoln knew that the men and women who had lived all their lives in slave cabins would need help building new lives for themselves. The 4 million freed slaves would be refugees of the war, without homes and with no way to earn a living. Lincoln realized that until a new order could be established the former slaves would need help obtaining food and medicine, finding the members of their scattered families, and educating their children. The president created an agency that would provide for those needs. In March 1865, Congress established the Bureau of Refugees, Freedmen, and Abandoned Lands, commonly called the Freedmen's Bureau.

When the war actually ended, however, the welfare of the former slaves was not the most pressing issue in the minds of most of the politicians. They were more concerned with how to reunite the country. The president, who was no longer Lincoln, and Congress had different ideas about how to reconstruct the Union and rebuild the defeated states.

# RESTORATION VERSUS RECONSTRUCTION

The president's plan was easy on Southern landowners. It granted amnesty to most Southerners. The president's plan allowed a state to come back into the Union when 10 percent of its voters pledged loyalty to the Union and agreed to the Thirteenth Amendment, which ended slavery. It said nothing about the status or rights of the former slaves; it left those matters up to each state. Andrew Johnson, who succeeded Abraham Lincoln, called his plan "restoration." Its goal was to restore the states to what they had been before the war.

The congressional plan, introduced by radical Republicans, had an entirely different goal. Congress wanted the South to be punished. The congressional plan was called "reconstruction." It demanded that 50 percent of the states' voters pledge loyalty. It also insisted that the former slaves be allowed to vote. This would change the balance of power in the House of Representatives. Before the war, the South had been largely Democratic. During and after the war, with eleven southern states out of the Union, Republicans held the majority in the House. Readmission of the eleven states would bring the southern Democrats back to Congress. Before the Thirteenth Amendment, the number of representatives for each state had been determined by counting a slave as three fifths of a person. Now that slaves were free, they would each count as one person. This would give the South thirteen to twenty additional representatives. The only way the radicals could maintain their majority in Congress was to ensure that those new representatives were Republican. If they championed the cause of African Americans being allowed to vote, they could persuade them to vote Republican. Their main interest was not African Americans or the welfare of the South, but maintaining Republican rule.

In 1866, the congressional plan for reconstruction won out over the presidential plan because the radicals had more supporters than the president. The radical Republicans imposed military rule over the formerly rebellious states until the states wrote new constitutions acceptable to Congress. To maintain control over the progress of the South, the radicals formed a coalition of three groups. One group consisted of Southerners who had not wanted their states to leave the Union. Southern Democrats called them *scalawags*, meaning "worthless people."

People who had come from the North to the South at the end of the Civil War formed the second group. Their critics called them *carpetbaggers*. This term implied that they were poor people (which they were not) who traveled south with their few possessions in suitcases made of carpet pieces. The third group in the radical Republican coalition was made up of the former slaves. Without their 725,000 votes, the people who had seceded from the Union might have written the states' constitutions.[1] To gain their votes, the Republicans made sure that some African Americans had positions in the newly forming governments.

Section 2. All freedmen, free negroes and mulattoes . . . over the age of eighteen years, found . . . with no lawful employment or business, or found unlawfully assembling themselves together . . . and all white persons assembling themselves with freedmen, Free negroes or mulattoes, or usually associating with freedmen, free negroes or mulattoes, on terms of equality, or living in adultery or fornication with a freed woman, freed negro or mulatto, shall be . . . fined and [imprisoned] at the discretion of the court . . .[2]

During Reconstruction, fourteen African Americans served in the House of Representatives and two in the Senate.

# LAWS FOR AFRICAN AMERICANS

Even though blacks held very few elective offices, most white Southerners resented what they saw as "black rule." These whites put their prejudices into laws that severely limited the freedoms of blacks. The laws, called Black Codes, differed from state to state.

Entered according to act of Congress in the year 1872 by Currier & Ives, in the Office of the Librarian of Congress at Washington
ROBERT C. DE LARGE, M.C. of S.Carolina.      JEFFERSON H. LONG, M.C. of Georgia
U.S. Senator H.R.REVELS, of Mississippi.   BENJ. S. TURNER, M.C. of Alabama.      JOSIAH T. WALLS, M.C. of Florida.      JOSEPH H. RAINY, M.C. of S.Carolina.   R. BROWN ELLIOT, M.C. of S.Carolina.

THE FIRST COLORED SENATOR AND REPRESENTATIVES,
In the 41st and 42nd Congress of the United States.

NEW YORK, PUBLISHED BY CURRIER & IVES, 125 NASSAU STREET.

During Reconstruction, the process of putting the country back together, African-American men played a part in legislation, holding positions in Congress.

In some states, freedmen could hold jobs only on other people's farms or as servants. They had to have special licenses to do anything but work on a farm. They could not buy or rent any farmland; they could live only in towns and cities. Any African American found without a job could be arrested, fined, and put in prison. If he could not pay the fine, the sheriff could hire him out to any person who could pay the fine.

Some states required freedmen to sign one-year contracts for their labor. This locked them in to that employer for the entire year. If they left their workplace, they could be hunted down, brought back, and forced to work.

The Black Codes barred African Americans from nearly every political and social right. They prohibited them from voting, from

This 1872 political cartoon by Thomas Nast shows politicians forcing a black man to shake hands with KKK members. Racist whites desperately wanted to maintain control of their country.

carrying firearms, and from serving on juries. They refused them the right to bring testimony against whites. They imposed curfews and forbade marriage with nonblacks. As John Trowbridge, a Northerner, observed, the purpose of the Black Codes was "to place both the labor and the [black] laborer in the power of the [white] employer, and to reorganize slavery under a new name."[3]

# COUNTERING THE BLACK CODES

The radical Republicans attempted to nullify the effects of the Black Codes. The codes were state laws, so Congress could not declare them invalid. Congress could, however, make national laws that overrode the state codes. And it could refuse to readmit the states to the Union until they agreed to the national legislation.

The radicals passed a law over President Johnson's veto extending the life and power of the Freedmen's Bureau. The bureau had been authorized to operate for only one year. The new law, together with later ones, kept the agency operating through 1869. Its purpose, however, shifted. Instead of providing for the physical needs of the freedmen, it protected the rights the Republicans wanted them to have. It helped African-American workers obtain reasonable wages and working conditions. It set up special courts that tried labor disputes. Often it got rid of the unfair work contracts that had been made under the Black Codes.

The radicals passed another law, again over the president's veto, to ensure African Americans' civil and political rights. The Civil Rights Act of 1866 declared that anyone born in the United States—with the exception of American Indians—was a US citizen. The law specified that citizens "of every race and color" had the same rights in every state. They could sue and testify in court, and they could buy and sell property.[4] Perhaps more importantly, a black man could vote.

Opposition to the Civil Rights Act was strong in the North as well as the South. Many northern states had laws against blacks marrying whites, serving on juries, and voting. The radicals, who needed the black vote, were afraid the Supreme Court might declare the 1866 act unconstitutional. So, they wrote most of the provisions of the law into a constitutional amendment. Then they ruled that the former Confederate states had to ratify the amendment before being allowed back into the Union.

The Fourteenth Amendment established that anyone born in the United States (and any foreigner who had become a citizen) was entitled to all the privileges and protections of the law. It did not specify, however, what those privileges and protections were. It mentioned voting only indirectly, punishing any state that denied its citizens the right to vote by reducing its number of representatives in the House.

For the most part, the voting measure of the Fourteenth Amendment was ignored. So, Congress proposed another that was very clear. The Fifteenth Amendment stated plainly, "The right of citizens of the United States to vote shall not be denied or abridged by the United States or by any State on account of race, color, or previous condition of servitude." Southerners were strongly opposed to the amendment, and many Northern states refused to ratify it. It became law in 1870 only because four Southern states were forced to ratify it to be readmitted to the Union.

The mere existence of laws affirming the rights of freedmen did not guarantee that they could exercise those rights. Racist Southerners (and Northerners) had ways of getting around the laws.

# INTIMIDATION AND TERROR

A number of terrorist organizations arose in the Reconstruction South that used violence and intimidation against African Americans. The largest and most well known was the Ku Klux Klan (KKK).

The Klan did not start as an instrument of terrorism. It began in Tennessee on December 24, 1865. Six officers of the disbanded Confederate army joined in a circle of friends. They took their name from the Greek word for circle, *kuklos*.

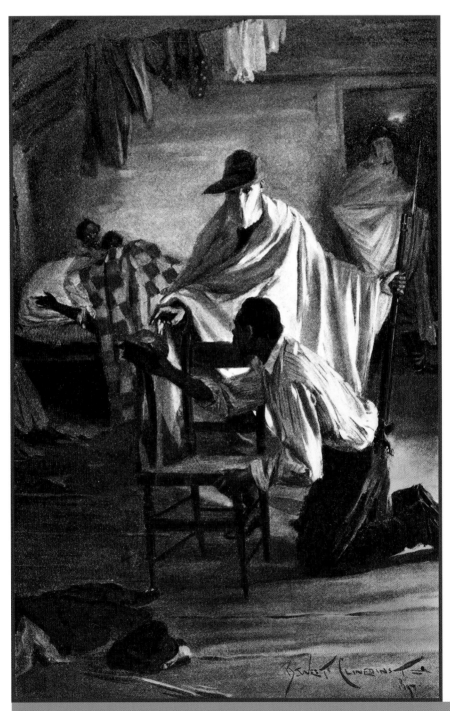

The Ku Klux Klan ran a campaign of terror against African Americans. The Klan usually included powerful members of the community, so there were few consequences for their actions.

The circle grew larger at the same time African Americans were making political and economic gains. The KKK began to do what it could to reverse those gains. Its members disrupted meetings of Republicans and tried to frighten African Americans into silence.

The growing group spread across several states. In 1867, in a secret convention in Nashville, the Klan was formally organized. The organization's stated purposes were to "protect the weak, the innocent, and the defenseless" and "defend the Constitution of the United States."

In order to defend their interpretation of the Constitution, members had to swear that they were "opposed to negro [a term for African Americans at the time] equality, both social and political" and "in favor of a white man's government."[5]

Defending the "white man's government" meant opposing black men who tried to raise themselves to anything approaching equality with whites. At first, the KKK threatened and frightened African Americans. Klansmen disguised themselves with white robes or sheets, masks, and pointed hoods. They rode horses draped in white to give a ghostly appearance. They surrounded homes of blacks they thought were trying to be "as good as" whites. Sometimes they burned crosses near their homes to add to the fear. Eventually, some of the KKK destroyed African-Americans' property, beat them, and killed many.

The first Grand Wizard, former Confederate general Nathan Bedford Forrest, denied that the KKK had any political purpose. Despite that claim, the all-white KKK kept huge numbers of blacks from voting. Its violence against African Americans grew so fierce that Forrest disbanded the organization in 1869. Even without a central command, however, local groups of Klansman continued to operate for three more years. Three laws, federal troops, and hundreds of arrests finally brought much of the terrorism to an end.

But by that time, employment, property, and voting protections for African Americans were ignored in the South. Still, one of the achievements of Reconstruction remained and held promise: free public education for African Americans.

African-American children and adults stand outside a Freedmen's school in South Carolina. The Freedmen's Bureau encouraged achievement through education, hard work, and self-sufficiency.

# SCHOOLS FOR AFRICAN-AMERICAN CHILDREN

The Freedmen's Bureau invested more than $5 million in schools for Southern African Americans.[6] The Bureau purchased buildings. Charitable societies in the North sent teachers and books. In 1870, four thousand schools were in operation with two hundred thousand students. By 1876, 40 percent of the black children of the South were in school.[7]

The director of the Freedmen's Bureau, General Oliver Howard, believed that education of African Americans was "the true relief . . . from . . . dependence."[8] He also felt that colleges for African Americans were necessary. A few universities for African Americans were located in the North. However, Howard wanted to see them in the South, where the majority of African Americans lived. And he was successful. African-American colleges were established in Georgia, Tennessee, Virginia, and Washington, D.C.

None of these schools, from primary to university, was built for African Americans only. They were free public schools, open to everyone. But most whites refused to send their children to classrooms with blacks. African Americans were legally free, but they were not treated as equals.

# CHAPTER 3

# SEPARATE IS NOT EQUAL: 1877–1915

The attitudes and customs of decades that separated blacks and whites in almost all everyday activities were not quickly changed. According to law, blacks and whites in America were equal politically. In actual practice, however, whites had advantages and opportunities that blacks did not. This was especially evident throughout the South. And many whites, particularly in the South, believed they had a right, and even a duty, to maintain those advantages. In addition to attitudes, economics kept blacks in the South from achieving the same status as whites. Black sharecroppers and farm laborers were dependent on their white employers for their livelihoods. Thus, for many years after Reconstruction, segregation continued as it had before the Civil War.

However, two factors threatened white supremacy in the South: the Reconstruction laws that gave blacks equal rights and the movement of blacks from the farms to the cities.

# EQUAL UNDER THE LAW

By the time federal troops left the South in 1877, all the governments of the former Confederacy had been "redeemed"—they were back in the hands of whites. The white rulers desperately wanted to deprive blacks of the political power they had won in the previous ten years. Most whites wanted to legalize the informal segregation that existed in rural areas. They wanted to protect the economic system that kept them on top.

But federal laws made dismantling the political effects of Reconstruction difficult. The Fourteenth Amendment had made the former slaves United States citizens. The Fifteenth Amendment forced the Southern governments to allow black men to vote. The Civil Rights Acts of 1866 and 1875 made racial discrimination illegal. To "undo" Reconstruction, Southern governments needed to figure out how to get around these laws.

# THE LURE OF THE CITY

But the laws were only half the problem. Maintaining the old economic system was also hindered by the migration of African Americans from the countryside to urban centers.

The cities of the South were enticing to rural African Americans. They offered an escape from the field work they associated with slavery. And they offered jobs. The South was becoming rapidly industrialized, and new plants and factories needed workers.

In the mills and on the streets of these cities, blacks and whites were in closer and more frequent contact than in the rural areas. The owner/tenant relationship that kept blacks under and separate from whites on the farms did not exist in the cities. The old ways of relating did not work. African Americans responded to the change by building their own communities. They lived together in African-American neighborhoods and worshipped in African-American churches. Some built African-American businesses. Whites, still trying to assert their superiority, created separate facilities for blacks. The nicer schools, washrooms, and drinking fountains, for example, were for whites only. The poorer ones could be used by blacks.

The whites found, however, that the blacks—in both urban and rural areas—were not as easily dominated as they had been under slavery. So Southern governments tried harder to reassert the master/servant order. They began by devising ways to keep African Americans from voting.

# BARRIERS TO VOTING

The Fifteenth Amendment to the Constitution guaranteed the franchise (voting privilege) to every African-American man. State governments could not tell African Americans they could not vote. But nothing in the amendment forbade them from placing qualifications for voting on all their citizens. States set age limits for voting; why not set other restrictions? As long as the requirements were demanded of everyone, the conditions of the law were met. Immediately after Reconstruction ended, Southern leaders erected barriers to voting that were technically "equal" but separated blacks from whites.

One barrier was the poll tax. In most Southern states, voters had to pay a tax in order to vote. It was called a *poll tax* because it supposedly went to pay for the polls—the places where people voted. Since most African Americans were sharecroppers, they operated with little or no cash. They could not afford even a small tax.

For those who could pay the poll tax, a property requirement could bar them from the polls. This restriction required that, in order to vote, a person had to own property. If that was not enough to keep blacks from voting, some states required vouchers: an already registered voter (usually a white person) had to vouch for a new voter, saying that he lived in the district or was of "good character." Few if any African Americans could obtain a voucher.

EDDIKASHUN
QUALIFUKASHUN.
·
THE BLAKMAN ORTER
BE EDDIKATED AFORE
HE KIN VOTE WITH
US WITES.

MR. SOLID SOUTH

This political cartoon satirizes the irony of the barriers laid down by whites to keep blacks from voting. The illustration suggests that many whites were not any more educated than former slaves.

Probably the largest and most unequal voting restriction was the literacy test. At first, this exam forced people to demonstrate that they could read and understand the ballot. But in 1890, Mississippi added a twist that other states quickly adopted. The new literacy test required that, in order to vote, applicants had to be able to read and interpret the federal and state constitutions. The test included questions such as:

- The Constitution limits the size of the District of Columbia to what?
- When the Constitution was approved by the original colonies, how many had to ratify it in order for it to be in effect?
- Persons opposed to swearing an oath may say instead, "I solemnly _____"?
- If it were proposed to join Alabama and Mississippi to form one state, what groups would have to vote approval for this to be done?[1]

Most citizens would not be able to pass such a literacy test, so how did it keep African Americans from voting? It was administered by white voting registrars (people who signed voters up). They could give the test any way they wanted. They could give a test with easy questions to white applicants and a hard test to black applicants.

Some white Southerners could not pass the simplest literacy test. However, to weaken the voice of any African Americans who did manage to vote, all whites had to be enfranchised. To ensure that illiterate or poor whites could vote, some states passed laws with "grandfather clauses." These stated that anyone whose grandfather had voted before the Fifteenth Amendment became law (in 1870) had the right to vote. This, of course, applied only to whites, for no black man voted in the South before Reconstruction.

Not one of these measures directly violated the Fifteenth Amendment. Yet they kept African Americans from voting. In South Carolina, for example, 70 percent of African-American men voted in 1890. But in 1896, after these voting restrictions were fully in place, only 10 percent voted.[2]

For those few Southern African Americans who could vote, however, life was little different from what it had been under slavery. Their vote could not change the fact that, socially, they were still separate from and subordinate to whites.

> What do you want? You tried the infamous eight-box [required poorly educated voters to place ballots correctly in eight separate ballot boxes, one for each office] and registration laws until they were worn to such a thinness that they could stand neither the test of the law nor of public opinion. [On] behalf of the 600,000 negroes in the State and the 132,000 negro voters all that I demand is that a fair and honest election law be passed.[3]

# LEGALIZING SEPARATION

Even after emancipation, blacks and whites in the South lived separately. No law was needed to enforce segregation because no other option was open to many Southern African Americans. But the concentration of blacks in Southern cities and the brief taste of power some blacks had during Reconstruction challenged the racial inequality. The majority of Southern whites feared that mixing the races in any way would "bring down" the white race. To enforce racial separation, a series of laws was enacted primarily in the South from the 1880s through 1910. These measures were named after the fictitious Jim Crow.

Jim Crow was the name of a character in a minstrel show. Minstrel shows were traveling song-and-dance performances. The performers were white men who blackened their faces and hands with charcoal or burnt cork and made fun of African Americans. The laws that solidified segregation throughout the South eventually became known as Jim Crow laws.

Jim Crow laws were established to enforce segregation. The separate facilities, including schools, water fountains, restrooms, and restaurants, were supposed to be "equal" but rarely were.

These laws regulated blacks wherever they went. They called for separate train cars for whites and blacks, separate waiting rooms, and separate ticket windows. Every public place that admitted blacks was required to have a separate door for them. Blacks and whites could not use the same telephone booths or drinking fountains. Even black and white juvenile delinquents had to be in "separate buildings, not nearer than one fourth mile to each other."[4] The Jim Crow laws segregated

the races in education and entertainment; parks and prisons; libraries and lunchrooms; baseball, barbershops, and bathrooms. Even in death, blacks could not be buried in the same cemeteries as whites.

# TAKING THE LAWS TO COURT

African Americans fought these unjust, oppressive laws. They challenged Jim Crow by breaking the laws and forcing the courts to rule on whether the state laws violated their rights by going against federal laws. Their only hope lay in the courts declaring the individual statutes unconstitutional.

This image of a crowded and shabby African-American classroom depicts the resources that were anything but "equal" to those "separate" schools attended by white children.

But the courts were not sympathetic to African Americans. In 1883, the US Supreme Court received five complaints of discrimination in public places. The African Americans who sued claimed that the treatment they had received violated the Civil Rights Act of 1875. This law guaranteed that "all persons" were entitled to "full and equal enjoyment" of any public accommodation. Instead of siding with the African Americans, the court decided that the Civil Rights Act was unconstitutional. Chief Justice Joseph Bradley ruled that the Fourteenth Amendment kept states from discriminating in political matters but did not prohibit private businesses and individuals from discriminating in social affairs.

Disappointed but not defeated, those against segregation tried again in 1896. They tested a Louisiana law that required that African Americans ride in separate railroad cars. A light-skinned man named Homer Plessy got on a train—and sat in the car for whites. He was arrested and convicted of breaking the state law. Plessy appealed, arguing that he was denied the protection of the Fourteenth Amendment.

The Supreme Court agreed with the lower court. The justices ruled in *Plessy v. Ferguson* that Plessy's rights were not violated just because he was refused admittance to the car for whites. As long as there was a car he could ride in, he had rights equal to those of any white passenger. The accommodation for him was separate, but it was equal. And to the court, "separate but equal" was fair.

African Americans knew better. Their separate accommodations were seldom equal to those of whites. Nevertheless, the separate-but-equal doctrine of segregation remained the law of the land for the next fifty-eight years.

Three years after the *Plessy v. Ferguson* decision, a case arose in Georgia. This time the separate accommodations were obviously not equal. African-American citizens were required to pay taxes to support schools. However, the only high school their children were allowed to attend had been closed down. So, they paid for schools but had no school for their own children. In *Cumming v. Richmond County Board of Education,* the Supreme Court ruled that closing the school for African Americans did not deny "equal protection of the laws or of any privileges belonging to [African Americans] as citizens" and was not "a clear and unmistakable disregard of [their] rights."[5] So, "separate but equal," in practice, simply meant separate. Segregation had been sanctioned by the highest court in the land.

# GOING BEYOND THE LAW

But segregation was not enough for many whites. So they resorted to a tactic their forefathers had used—brutality. Slave owners had whipped and even killed African Americans; the children of slave owners lynched them. When powerful white people wanted to get rid of blacks, they accused them of serious crimes—usually murder or rape. Then they hanged them or burned them alive without a trial.

The lynchings were usually public spectacles. People often came great distances to witness them, bringing picnic lunches and cheering.[6] Sometimes the victims were guilty, but more often the charges were false. Either way, the victim was not given a fair trial, as required by the United States Constitution. No one knows the actual number of people lynched, but at least 4,742 cases between 1882 and 1968 are recorded.[7] The majority took place in the South in the 1890s.

African Americans were divided on how to deal with the injustices to which they were subjected. Of the many voices attempting to guide them, those of two men offered opposing advice—Booker T. Washington and W.E.B. Du Bois.

# VOICE OF A FORMER SLAVE

Booker T. Washington was born a slave nine years before emancipation. He later helped found Tuskegee Institute in Alabama, a technical training college for African Americans. He worked himself up from slavery to college president through determination and persistence, and he encouraged other African Americans to do the same. He felt that fighting for their rights would get them nowhere. He wanted them to pursue education and jobs. Washington thought that being economically self-reliant was more important than being socially or politically equal. "The opportunity to earn a dollar in a factory just now," he said, "is worth infinitely

Booker T. Washington worked his way from slavery to a college presidency. Washington believed that the key to success for African Americans was education, employment, and self-reliance.

more than the opportunity to spend a dollar in an opera-house."[8] In a speech that made him famous, he urged his people, "Cast down your bucket where you are."[9] By this, he meant they should not protest their circumstances, but work their way out of them.

The white people of the South were pleased that Washington advised his people to work hard, wait patiently, and not make trouble. Many African Americans admired Washington. But some African-American leaders criticized him. One was W.E.B. Du Bois.

# VOICE OF A NORTHERN BLACK

Unlike Washington, Du Bois was never a slave. Born in Massachusetts three years after emancipation, he lived in a largely white community. He was the first African American to receive a Ph.D. from Harvard. He did not experience the indignities of Jim Crow until he went to the South as a young adult. Du Bois felt that Washington encouraged African Americans to accept an inferior position. He, on the other hand, called for them to pressure for full equality. He looked to the brightest and most educated African Americans, the ones he called the "talented tenth." By this, he meant the top 10 percent. He thought they could achieve justice for all. He and seven white men headed the National Association for the Advancement of Colored People (NAACP). In its early years, the NAACP fought against lynchings and brought civil rights cases to court.

# MORE PEOPLE SPEAK OUT

Other African-American voices emerged in the period following Recon-struction. A number of authors wrote of their own or others' experiences during and after slavery. In *The Colored Cadet at West Point*, Henry Ossian Flipper told what life was like for the first African American at the military academy. The escaped slave Frederick Douglass, who fought against slavery for more than twenty years, wrote his autobiography. Sarah Bradford published the story of Harriet Tubman, heroine of the

Underground Railroad. Ida B. Wells, a crusading editor of an African-American newspaper, documented violence and injustice against her people.

African-American fiction also blossomed. William Wells Brown and Charles Chesnutt wrote novels and short stories that described life in the South. James Madison Bell, Albery A. Whitman, and Frances E. W. Harper produced powerful poems, novels, and essays. The most famous African-American writer of the time was Paul Laurence Dunbar. Many have called him the "poet laureate of the Negro race."[10] Dunbar's poems and short stories captured the spirit of African Americans at the end of the nineteenth century. His words and verse depicted the hopes and hardships of their lives.

In his popular poem "Sympathy," Paul Laurence Dunbar uses the metaphor of a bird imprisoned in a cage to describe the plight and feelings of African Americans in the early 1900s.

*I know why the caged bird sings, ah me,*
*When his wing is bruised and his bosom sore,--*
*When he beats his bars and he would be free;*
*It is not a carol of joy or glee,*
*But a prayer that he sends from his heart's deep core,*
*But a plea that upward to Heaven he flings—*
*I know why the caged bird sings!*[11]

The South in the 1890s and 1900s was a difficult place for African Americans. They had the right to vote, but they could not register to exercise that right. They were free to move about, but where they could go was restricted. Under the Constitution, they were full-fledged citizens, but no court protected their rights or their lives. For many Southern African Americans, life was much the same as it had been under slavery.

# CHAPTER 4

# ACCOMPLISHMENT IS NOT EQUALITY: 1915–1941

Despite the oppression of Jim Crow throughout the South as well as the intimidation of white mobs, the former "slave states" were home to almost 90 percent of all blacks in the United States in 1900.[1] Many African Americans knew, or at least hoped, that their prospects for a better life were greater in the cities of the North or the West. In the short period between 1910 and 1920, about fifty thousand African Americans made their way out of the South each year.[2]

The desire to flee injustice and violence were not the only factors driving them north. Economic difficulties also propelled them. The boll weevil, an insect, had devastated the cotton fields of the South. Floods had ruined other crops. Neither farmers nor sharecroppers could make a living, and most other jobs were closed to African Americans. Many were drawn north by the promise of jobs that were opened up as a result of World War I.

# WARTIME ACHIEVEMENTS

When the United States entered the war in 1917, it had to manufacture planes, guns, and bombs. Many of the men who usually worked in the manufacturing plants were in Europe fighting the war. Manufacturers needed laborers and were willing to hire African Americans.

At the same time, the government needed soldiers. So the army and the navy opened its enlistment rolls to all male citizens. And 370,000 African-American men volunteered.[3] They fought bravely; many gave their lives in battle.

However, they did not find equality in the military; blacks were not allowed to mix with whites. The Marines would not even admit African Americans. Only about half the African-American soldiers were allowed to fight; the rest worked in noncombatant positions.[4] American General Pershing sent orders to French officers not to allow the French men to mix with African-American soldiers. "We cannot deal with them on the same plane as with the white American . . . " the orders stated. "We must not eat with them, must not shake hands or seek to talk or meet with them."[5]

For the most part, however, Europeans treated African Americans with dignity and gratitude, as equals. Although the US government did not recognize the valor of its African-American soldiers, the French government gave numerous awards to four all-black regiments.

African-American soldiers returned from the war with pride. They had served their country and the world well. They had witnessed racial equality from Europeans. They were not about to settle willingly for the inferior status they had in the United States. In the NAACP magazine *The Crisis*, W.E.B. Du Bois warned that African Americans were eager to defeat the enemy of racial injustice. He wrote, "We return from fighting. We return fighting."[6]

African Americans contributed to the war effort, including risk-
ing their lives in combat during the first and second World Wars.
However, they were subject to discrimination, just like at home.

Just a couple of decades later, blacks would find themselves representing their country once again in World War II. And, although slightly improved, once again they faced institutional racism. James A. Moss, commander of the 367th Infantry, an African-American regiment, said,

*Treat and handle the colored man as you would any other human being ... and you will have as good a soldier as history has ever known--a man who will drill well, shoot well, march well, obey well, fight well--in short, a man who will give a good account of himself in battle, and who will conduct and behave himself properly in camp, in garrison and in other places. I commanded colored troops ... and I have had some of them killed and wounded by my very side. At no time did they ever falter at the command to advance nor hesitate at the order to charge. I am glad that I am to command colored soldiers in this, my third campaign.*[7]

## CONFLICTS AT HOME

A different kind of fighting was taking place in America's cities. It had begun before the war in Europe ended. Competition for jobs had created tensions between black and white factory workers. In East St. Louis, Illinois, those tensions turned violent in 1917. White workers attacked a black neighborhood with guns and

Racial tensions culminated in the violent summer of 1919, dubbed the "Red Summer." Here, a group of white children celebrate after raiding and damaging an African-American home in Chicago.

torches, killing more than two hundred. Over the next few years, similar riots erupted in other cities.

The year 1919 was the bloodiest. Race wars broke out in twenty-six cities throughout both North and South. So many were killed and injured that African-American writer and NAACP secretary James Weldon Johnson called the summer of 1919 the "Red Summer."

The incident that set off the mob attacks usually had to do with a white person's perception that a black person had crossed the "color line." The color line was an invisible barrier erected by whites to keep blacks in their "place." The color line was everywhere, marking where people could live, what jobs they could hold, who they could talk to and how.

As African Americans moved to the cities and gained a small amount of personal freedom, the color line weakened. In the North, especially after the war, African Americans crossed the line to find better jobs and housing. For racist whites, the only way to keep the line intact was through intimidation and violence.

# THE KLAN RETURNS

White supremacists—people who declared openly that the white race was superior to all others—resorted to an old terror tactic. In 1915, they reorganized the KKK. In the same year, D. W. Griffith made a silent movie titled *Birth of a Nation* based on the best-selling book *The Clansman*. The film portrayed African Americans as childish, lazy, and vicious. It depicted Klansmen as heroes who saved the South from African-American rule during Reconstruction. The movie was so popular that people crowded in long lines to join the KKK. The new KKK had chapters in nearly every state of the union.

The KKK was dedicated to frightening everyone into accepting the supremacy of the white race. It boasted a membership as high as 2 or 3 million, including police officers and ministers.[8] Like the old KKK, members wore white robes and hoods. They burned crosses to scare people into submission. They often kidnapped, beat, and killed African Americans, Jews, Catholics, and others.

The activities of the KKK, the racial riots, the lynchings, and the continued discrimination made the early twentieth century a difficult time for black people in America.

# AN APPEAL TO SEPARATISM

One African-American leader tried to talk others into leaving America and forming their own country in Africa. Marcus Garvey came to New York in 1916 from the island of Jamaica. He invited other blacks to join his Universal Negro Improvement Association (UNIA). The main purpose of the association was to create a nation for African Americans in Africa. Garvey also wanted to establish schools "for the racial education and culture" of African Americans and "promote the spirit of pride and love."9

To accomplish these aims, UNIA built a number of black-owned businesses: grocery stores, laundries, restaurants, and small factories. It formed a shipping company called the Black Star Steamship Line. The steamships were to be used to ferry to Africa the two million followers Garvey claimed. UNIA published a weekly newspaper, the *African American World*. In 1920, Garvey organized a parade of fifty thousand and a convention of twenty-five thousand at Madison Square Garden in New York City. He traveled around the world, winning many to his cause with his flashy style and persuasive speech.

Looking forward a century or two, we can see an economic and political death struggle for the survival of the different race groups. . . . The fight for bread and position will be keen and severe. The weaker and unprepared group is bound to go under. That is why . . . we are fighting for the founding of a negro nation in Africa, so that there will be no clash between black and white and that each race will have a separate existence and civilization all its own without courting suspicion and hatred or eyeing each other with jealousy and rivalry. . .10

Marcus Garvey's radical ideas about creating a separate nation for African Americans served to awaken a sense of cultural pride in America's black population.

Garvey was a great speaker. However, he was convicted of mail fraud in 1923. After serving two years in prison, he was deported to Jamaica. His movement faded, but he had awakened a pride in being black. He had proclaimed to people who had been "put down" all their lives that "black is beautiful," that theirs was a "mighty race," and that they could accomplish whatever they wanted.[11]

# SELF-HELP ACHIEVEMENTS

For African Americans at that time, accomplishments were hard won. Most lived in the poorest sections of their cities. Their poorly funded schools did not give them good educations, which kept them from qualifying for good-paying jobs. And their poor-paying jobs held them in the poorest parts of town. The only way out of the cycle was to help one another.

African Americans' money was not accepted at white-owned banks, so they established their own banks. White-owned insurance companies would not sell them insurance, so they provided their own. There was

Being denied inclusion in the white establishment did not mean that African Americans didn't achieve. They simply created their own systems and businesses, such as the popular Negro Leagues.

no social service system to care for widows and other poor blacks, so black churches took care of such things. White-owned companies would not hire African Americans, so they started their own businesses. White-owned newspapers printed prejudiced articles, so African Americans produced their own newspapers. They built their own theaters after being excluded from white-owned theaters. White-owned baseball leagues refused to let blacks play, so blacks organized the Negro National League.

Created in response to racial exclusion, these organizations were a source of African-American pride and unity. That pride erupted in a cultural explosion known as the Harlem Renaissance.

# AFRICAN-AMERICAN ARTS

In the 1920s and 1930s, poets, writers, musicians, dancers, and actors gave eloquent voice to the African-American experience. This creative movement began in the cities of the North—mainly New York and

Artistic expression was a way of combatting oppression. Important contributions to music, art, and literature were made by African Americans during the Harlem Renaissance.

Chicago, but also Detroit and Kansas City. Most of the activity centered in the huge African-American community of New York City called Harlem. So this period of creative blossoming was called the Harlem Renaissance.

One of the first writers of the Harlem Renaissance was Claude McKay. One of his poems was published in *The Liberator*, a newspaper founded in 1831 by white antislavery leader William Lloyd Garrison. Written during the race riots and printed in 1919, "If We Must Die" reflected the agony and the determination of urban blacks:

> If we must die, let it not be like hogs
> Hunted and penned in an inglorious spot. . . .
> If we must die, O let us nobly die. . . .
> Like men we'll face the murderous, cowardly pack,
> Pressed to the wall, dying, but fighting back![12]

African-American writer Jean Toomer's novel *Cane* described the painful realities of life for African Americans in Georgia. Zora Neale Hurston wrote plainly about racism and black community life in Florida. Many other authors, such as Countee Cullen, James Weldon Johnson, and Arna Bontemps, also penned vivid portrayals of the joys and sufferings of their people. The most famous was Langston Hughes.

The Harlem Renaissance is probably best known for its music. When African Americans from the Mississippi delta, Memphis, and New Orleans came north, they brought with them their distinct musical forms. These included blues, spirituals, and the field songs of the South. In the slums of Harlem and Chicago, these forms were blended and transformed. With the brass instruments of New Orleans, the music was reworked and modernized. It spread through the entire country and became known as jazz.

Jazz was immensely popular with whites as well as blacks. Many wealthy white citizens came to the clubs and ballrooms of Harlem or Chicago's South Side to dance to the music of Louis "Satchmo" Armstrong, King Oliver, Duke Ellington, Cab Calloway, Chick Webb, Fletcher Henderson,

Jelly Roll Morton, and Count Basie. In some of those clubs, blacks and whites rubbed shoulders on the same dance floors.

But white acceptance was generally limited to black art, not black people. As in the days of slavery, African Americans could serve whites— could entertain them—but could not socialize with them. Many of the famous clubs allowed African Americans in only on designated nights and at specified times. W. C. Handy, the great composer of "St. Louis Blues" and other popular songs, was not permitted to enter the Cotton Club on the evening his music was being celebrated.[13] "Separate but equal" was still the law of the land.

# CHAPTER 5

# GAINING GROUND: 1941–1965

Although "separate but equal" was the expressed policy for the country in the 1930s, economic opportunities were obviously not equal. The hardships of the Great Depression fell heavily on African Americans. They were nearly always the first to be laid off. Black unemployment was two or three times the rate for whites.[1] With millions out of work, African Americans had almost no chance of landing any of the very few jobs available. The employment situation was so dire that Congress created programs that put people to work.

At the beginning, the public service programs demonstrated that "equal" still did not mean "the same as" whites. Wages for black workers were often lower than for white workers in the same job. Some of the programs would not accept African Americans. But as the depression worsened and the need grew more intense, the government programs addressed the economic condition of African Americans. The Works Progress Administration (WPA) and the Civilian Conservation Corp (CCC) offered employment and education opportunities to blacks as well as whites. The real turning point in seeing fair treatment and equality of rights, however, came with World War II.

# WAR BRINGS OPPORTUNITIES

Even before the United States entered the war, American companies produced materials for the country's allies. But when African Americans applied for jobs making war materials, they were denied that opportunity. Plenty of white men had been out of work, but African Americans also needed employment. By the time war production started, they had become bolder in asserting themselves. Early in 1941, African-American labor leader A. Philip Randolph met with President Franklin Roosevelt about discrimination in the defense industries.

Randolph knew the power of unity. Years before, he had organized African-American workers into a labor union, the Brotherhood of Sleeping Car Porters and Maids. He had won higher wages for eight thousand African-American workers. Now he had the backing of even more. He gave Roosevelt until July 1 to give African Americans the same chance to work in the war industries as whites—or one hundred thousand black men would stage a protest march in Washington. President Roosevelt could not risk the possibility of massive work stoppages and race riots while he was preparing for war. On June 21, less than a week before Randolph's deadline, he issued Executive Order 8802. It declared that "there shall be no discrimination in the employment of workers in defense industries or government because of race, creed, color or national origin."[2]

Once employment in the defense plants opened to African Americans, they flooded the factories and docks of New York, Chicago, Los Angeles, and San Francisco. Every year between 1940 and 1959, more than one hundred fifty thousand African Americans left the South.[3] When they

The Tuskegee Airmen were the US military's first African-American pilots. Despite an exemplary combat record in World War II, the airmen were racially harassed and discriminated against.

The defense industry did not appreciate Roosevelt's executive order. Here are some of the responses of war industry companies to calls to employ African Americans.

*"Negroes will be considered only as janitors. It is the company policy not to employ them as mechanics and aircraft workers."* —North American Aviation.

*"We have not had a Negro working in 25 years and do not plan on starting now."* — Standard Steel

*"It is not the policy of this company to employ other than of the Caucasian race."* —Vultee Air*[4]*

reached the cities where the jobs were, they were met by hostile whites. The whites resented having to compete with blacks for jobs and housing. Racial tensions led to full-scale riots.

Bigger battles, however, were taking place against a foreign enemy. In December 1941, the United States entered World War II. Three million African-American men registered to fight. But the idea persisted that the African American was inferior. Government leaders did not want African-American soldiers, but could not deny them the right to enlist. So, they limited the number that could join the armed services. African Americans made up 10 percent of the population of the country, so the government decided they could be no more than 10 percent of the fighting force. Of the 3 million who tried to register, only 1 million were allowed to serve.

Once in the military, they served in segregated units, and they ate and slept in separate quarters. Their squadrons were sent to training camps in the southern states, where discrimination often turned violent. Yet they fought valiantly and helped win a war in which prejudice (against Jews) was a big issue. They came home determined to win their own war against racial discrimination.

The first place to start was the segregation in the military. Again, A. Philip Randolph took the lead, threatening a massive protest demonstration. In 1948, by Executive Order 9981, President Harry Truman ended segregation in the armed forces.

# GAINING GROUND IN SPORTS

The previous year, another form of "separate but equal" was challenged. As in practically all areas of public life, African Americans had been barred from professional baseball. They had formed their own teams and joined them into the Negro National League. The league was successful, with forty-five thousand fans watching its first world series in 1924.[5]

In fact, African-American baseball was so successful that Branch Rickey, manager of the white Brooklyn Dodgers, took notice. He wondered if adding an African-American player to his team could boost attendance at the Dodgers' games and raise their profits. He signed one of the best players in the Negro League onto his team, a second baseman named Jackie Robinson.

Robinson played his first game for Brooklyn in 1947. He was an exceptional athlete. In 1949, he had the highest batting average in the National League and was named its Most Valuable Player.

But that was not enough to convince people that a black man could be "just as good as" a white. On and off the field, Robinson was harassed and ridiculed. People called him unkind names, yelled ugly things at him, and sometimes threw things at him. Even some of his teammates belittled him. He had crossed the color line, but he had not erased it.

17 million Negroes cannot do as you suggest and wait for the hearts of men to change. We want to enjoy now the rights that we feel we are entitled to as Americans. This we cannot do unless we pursue aggressively goals which all other Americans achieved over 150 years ago.

*As the chief executive of our nation, I respectfully suggest that you unwittingly crush the spirit of freedom in Negroes by constantly urging forbearance and give hope to those pro-segregation leaders like Governor Faubus who would take from us even those freedoms we now enjoy.*[6]

— Letter from Jackie Robinson to President Eisenhower

The line was weakening, however. It was weakening because African Americans, particularly in the North, had determined that it would come down. They had built up some economic and political strength and had learned how to use the power of their numbers. They were ready to go on the offensive.

# GAINING GROUND IN SCHOOLS

In the 1940s and 1950s, the major battleground for equal rights was public education. For years, the NAACP had tried to get the government to admit that the separate schools for blacks were not equal to the schools for whites. In 1950, the Topeka, Kansas, NAACP devised a new challenge.

Topeka had eighteen schools for whites and four schools for blacks. The African-American schools were far from their homes and not as nice or as well equipped as the schools for whites. Thirteen black parents attempted to enroll their twenty children in the white schools. When all twenty children were refused admittance, the NAACP sued the Topeka Board of Education.

At the same time, the NAACP was challenging school districts in Delaware, Virginia, South Carolina, and the District of Columbia. They filed suits as test cases. The African-American parents were testing the law, hoping the judges would say the law was unconstitutional. In all but one instance, the courts ruled that the school boards were justified in denying enrollment to the African-American children. Those children had separate but equal schools available to them according to most of the courts.

But the parents argued that their schools were not equal, that "separate" could never be "equal." They appealed to the Supreme Court, saying the lower courts' decisions violated their Fourteenth Amendment rights. The Supreme Court combined all the cases together in what became one of the most important judicial actions in the quest for civil rights: the 1954 case of *Brown v. Board of Education of Topeka, Kansas*.

The judges examined the 1896 *Plessy v. Ferguson* decision and ruled unanimously that its "doctrine of 'separate but equal'" that had been in force for fifty-eight years had "no place" in "public education." Chief Justice Earl Warren wrote:

> To separate [children] from others of similar age and qualifications solely because of their race generates a feeling of inferiority... that may affect their hearts and minds in a way unlikely ever to be undone.... Segregation of white and colored children in public schools has a detrimental effect upon the colored children.... Separating the races is usually interpreted as denoting the inferiority of the [African American] group.... Separate educational facilities are inherently unequal.[7]

The ruling was a huge victory for civil rights. It was an admission that the very act of separating people by ethnicity declared that one race was superior to another. It meant that no public school could turn away an African-American child.

But the ruling, made by federal judges, had to be enforced by the states. And some of the states of the Deep South did not want to desegregate, or integrate, anything. The Supreme Court ordered that states begin the process of integrating their schools "with all deliberate speed"—as quickly as possible. For some southern states, "all deliberate speed" meant years. One of those states was Arkansas.

# GOVERNORS PROTEST

Three years after the *Brown* decision, the schools in Little Rock, Arkansas, were still segregated. Arkansas NAACP president Daisy Bates worked with the school board to integrate the city's schools gradually. They would begin with only nine African-American students in one school. However, when the students tried to enter Central High School in 1957, they were blocked. An angry white crowd stood in their way. With the crowd were the state's governor and soldiers of the National Guard carrying rifles and bayonets.

After a ten-day standoff, Governor Orval Faubus relented. He promised President Dwight Eisenhower that he would not only admit the "Little Rock Nine" to the school, but would also order the National Guard to protect them. Instead, he dismissed the soldiers and left the students to make their own way through the hostile mob. The angry citizens yelled and spat at the youths. They beat a number of reporters and hurled bricks through the school's windows and doors. City police had to escort the students out at the end of the school day.

All this was broadcast on national television. People were outraged, and Eisenhower put the Arkansas National Guard under his command. He sent twelve hundred armed paratroopers to the scene. Under federal protection, the nine finished the school year as the first African-American students in the Arkansas public schools.

Although the integration of Central High School was a major victory for all African Americans, it was a nightmare for those first nine students. Their white peers followed them everywhere, taunting them and calling them names. One teacher kept her classroom segregated, seating the blacks away from the whites.[8]

Students in other states and other schools had similar problems as states enforced the court's "all deliberate speed" mandate at a snail's pace. Three thousand federal troops were needed to admit one black man, James Meredith, to the University of Mississippi in 1962. In 1963, the president was again forced to send soldiers to the South when Governor George Wallace stood in the doorway of the University of Alabama to block the entrance of two African-American students.

Some governors tried to get around court-ordered integration by closing all public schools. Faubus closed Little Rock's school for a year. One county in Virginia closed its schools for four years. These districts opened private schools for whites only, which operated with state funds.[9] Even after schools were finally desegregated, many districts tried to keep African-American enrollment to a minimum. Little by little, however, through court orders, federal troops, and public pressure, all the public schools in the nation were integrated. Mississippi was the last to comply. The state integrated its classrooms in 1964, ten years after *Brown v. Board of Education*.

School integration attempts were met with anger and hatred. Soldiers had to be dispatched to escort the Little Rock Nine students into the all-white Central High School in Little Rock, Arkansas.

# ANOTHER CHILD IN THE FIGHT

In the struggle for school desegregation, children were on the front lines. In fact, children remained in the center of several of the contests for equality. A year after the *Brown v. Board of Education* decision, when the first battle was won, a fourteen-year-old African-American boy ignited a new firestorm. In August 1955, Emmet Till visited his aunt and uncle in Mississippi. He was from Chicago, where the color line was more blurred than in the South. In Mississippi, Emmet went into a little store where a young white woman stood behind the counter. Some said he simply spoke to the woman; others said he whistled. Whatever his action, it angered someone in the white community. A few hours later, two white men went to the home of Emmet's uncle and took the teenager away.

Eight days later, Emmet's body was found at the bottom of the Tallahatchie River. He had been brutally beaten and shot in the head. The young woman's husband and her brother-in-law, Roy Bryant and J.W. Milam, were arrested. An all-white jury proclaimed them innocent of any crime. Years later the pair admitted to the murder. Knowing they could not be tried again or punished, they told their story to *Look* magazine for four thousand dollars.

Emmet's mother told her story, too. She refused to hide her son's disfigured body in a closed casket. Instead, she made sure that photographs of her boy's mutilated corpse were printed in newspapers and magazines. She wanted the entire country to see what racism did to children.

The pictures and the reporting that accompanied them aroused great anger and outrage. Thousands of people came to Emmet's funeral in Chicago. As one civil rights worker explained, the incident "shook the foundations" of Mississippi life, "both black and white . . . because it said that even a child was not safe from racism, bigotry, and death."[10] The murder of Emmet Till strengthened the resolve of African Americans to fight for their constitutionally guaranteed civil rights.

# A WOMAN'S PROTEST

Just a few months after Mamie Till buried her son, another woman entered the battle, this time in Montgomery, Alabama. Montgomery was typical of many cities in the Deep South. Everything was segregated. Some buses had separate doors and all had separate seating sections. The front was for whites, the back for blacks.

On December 1, 1955, a forty-two-year-old African-American seamstress, Rosa Parks, got on one of those buses. She sat toward the front of the African-American section. As more people boarded the bus, the whites' seats filled up. The driver ordered the African Americans to move farther back. By law, blacks had to give their places to white passengers if the white bus riders had no other seats.

But Rosa refused to move. An African-American man offered her his seat. The bus driver tried to persuade her, and a police officer threatened her. But she would not budge. She was arrested for breaking the law and put in jail.

Parks' arrest was just what African-American leaders needed to spur others to action. They formulated a plan that, if it worked, would hit the city where it would hurt most—in the pocketbook. Most of the people who rode buses in Montgomery were African American. The leaders thought that if the city lost money because its African-American citizens were not riding buses, the city would change the way it treated African Americans. Fifty thousand flyers blanketed the city the day after Rosa Parks' arrest. The flyers called for all African Americans to boycott the buses—to not use them—for one day, December 5.

# MINISTERS LEAD THE FIGHT

Many of the people organizing the boycott were ministers. Since the days of slavery, the church had been very important in African-American life. It was a source of stability and unity. The church was also a place where people could find practical help. The church fed the hungry, cared for the widows, counseled the hurting. Churches were the center of social life for many. Nearly all African-American singers, speakers, and leaders of that time got their start in church. African Americans looked to their ministers for direction and leadership.

Ministers took charge of the Montgomery bus boycott. They elected as their leader Martin Luther King, Jr., pastor of Dexter Avenue Baptist Church. King was only twenty-six years old, but he was an excellent speaker. He was also committed to winning for his people the dignity and equality to which they were entitled. He was committed to winning without violence. Together with fellow minister Ralph Abernathy and others, King rallied the people around the idea of a bus boycott.

On December 5, Montgomery's buses were nearly empty. The boycott leaders were overjoyed. The African Americans of the city had united and cost the city the income from thirty thousand to forty thousand bus riders.[11]

The leaders made only three requests of the city: African-American passengers should be treated politely, blacks should have as many seats as whites, and some African Americans should be hired as bus drivers. Despite losing a good deal of money, the city refused to give in to these demands. So the boycott was extended. For 381 days, the African-American citizens of Montgomery did not ride the buses. They carpooled or walked. They rode "rolling taxis"—station wagons donated by churches. Some people even drove horse-drawn wagons.

In the end, it was not their economic power that won. It was their determination to stick to what they believed was just. The Supreme Court recognized that Alabama's bus segregation law violated the constitution and ordered the state of Alabama to integrate its transportation system.

Just as the freeing of the slaves came only after a bloody war, this legal victory did not come without great cost. Members of the KKK terrorized black neighborhoods. Bombs shattered the homes of Martin Luther King, Jr., and Ralph Abernathy. Two African-American churches were completely leveled and two others badly damaged by bombs. The violence destroyed seventy thousand dollars worth of property.[12]

But the civil rights leaders and the black community were willing to bear the cost. They had just begun to fight.

# NEW PLACES AND NEW WEAPONS

One weapon of protest in the early 1960s was the sit-in. The sit-in movement began in Greensboro, North Carolina. On February 1, 1960, four black college students sat down at a "whites-only" lunch counter at a Woolworth store and ordered coffee. They were ignored by the server, the store manager, and a nearby police officer. Even though other customers harassed them, they did not fight back. They sat at the counter until the store closed, and then they left. But they came back the next day, bringing nineteen others. Again they were ignored. The next day, eighty-five students sat at the counter. By the end of the week, the number was four hundred—several of them white.[13] The students refused to move until they were served, and the store employees refused to serve them. Every day, the store lost money.

The idea spread to other American cities. Sit-ins were staged in department stores and libraries, at skating rinks and beaches. Stand-ins were formed in front of theaters that would not admit African Americans. Swim-ins closed some public pools, and pray-ins were held in segregated churches. A similar type of nonviolent resistance was used on buses that traveled from state to state. As early as 1947, "freedom riders," black and white, rode the buses and refused to move from their seats.

Although those leading this charge for freedoms were committed to nonviolence, those opposing them resorted to savage attacks. Many of the demonstrators were beaten, some were killed, and some were arrested. In jail, they were often beaten again. One of the freedom ride buses was burned. But the quiet resistance was paying off. Throughout the entire country, "whites only" signs were coming down. The separate-but-equal laws that had been in force for sixty years were being struck down.

Changing the law, however, did not necessarily change practice. Many whites, especially in the South, clung stubbornly to the plantation mentality that blacks were by nature inferior. Despite the guarantees of the Fourteenth Amendment, and despite civil rights legislation passed in 1957 and 1960, these whites did everything they could to keep blacks from getting good-paying jobs and decent housing, from mixing with whites,

Freedom Riders sponsored by the Congress of Racial Equality (CORE) watch their bus burn. It was set afire by racist whites who met the group upon their arrival in Alabama, in 1961.

and from voting. Legal equality was good, but African Americans were not going to abandon the cause of civil rights until they achieved real equality. They would not stop fighting until they were treated "just the same as" white people.

# MARCHING FOR EQUALITY

A new fight for fair and equal treatment was begun in 1963, one hundred years after the Emancipation Proclamation. It started in Birmingham, Alabama. Martin Luther King, Jr., described Birmingham as "probably the most thoroughly segregated city in the United States."[14] The battle cry of the 1963 Civil Rights movement was "Freedom now!"

The protest in Birmingham was two-pronged. Citizens would conduct an economic boycott of businesses that refused to serve African Americans. And protesters would stage nonviolent marches to bring national attention to their plight. The city stopped the boycott by closing stores. City leaders tried to stop the demonstration by a court order. But Martin Luther King,

Jr., disregarded the order and kept marching. After he was arrested, he explained why he defied the law. In a letter he smuggled out of the Birmingham jail he wrote, "There are two types of laws: just and unjust. . . . One has a moral responsibility to disobey unjust laws."[15]

Disobeying the law brought severe consequences. More than three thousand were arrested and jailed, including hundreds of children. People watching the demonstrations from the sidewalks threw rocks at the marchers. Unnamed whites bombed black churches and other buildings. Birmingham police chief "Bull" Conner tried to break up the demonstrations with police dogs, high-pressure fire hoses, and electric cattle prods—all directed at the protesters.

Although the brutal images of snarling dogs attacking unarmed men, women, and children angered blacks and whites everywhere, public sympathy did not stop the violence. In Birmingham just a few months after the demonstration, four black girls were killed in their Sunday school classroom by a bomb planted by Ku Klux Klansmen. Two young men were shot to death. NAACP leader Medgar Evers was killed in his driveway in nearby Jackson.

# TAKING THE BATTLE TO WASHINGTON

African-American leaders took their protest to the national capital. They hoped to awaken all of America to the injustices in the South. They wanted everyone to be aware of the discrimination they had endured for well over three hundred years. They also hoped to stir up support for a civil rights bill that was being debated in Congress.

On August 28, 1963, more than two hundred thousand Americans poured into the streets of Washington, D.C. They came from all over the country. Black and white, they walked arm in arm from the Washington Monument to the Lincoln Memorial, singing "We Shall Overcome." Without even a hint of rioting, they stood in the hot sun and listened to the words of their leaders. A minister from Birmingham spoke, Mahalia Jackson sang, and A. Phillip Randolph— who had conceived the idea of protest marches more than twenty years earlier—addressed the crowd.

Americans gathered on the Washington Mall in 1963 to participate in the March on Washington, the historic civil rights rally where Martin Luther King, Jr. gave his inspiring "I Have a Dream" speech.

The final speech was delivered by Reverend Martin Luther King, Jr. "We must face the tragic fact," he told the crowd, "that the Negro is still not free." But he soon would be, he promised. "I have a dream," he said, that "the sons of former slaves and the sons of former slave owners will be able to sit down together at the table of brotherhood."

"Now is the time," he roared to the approving thousands. "Now is the time to rise from the dark and desolate valley of segregation to the sunlit path of racial justice."[16]

# MORE GROUND TO TAKE

But racial justice did not come as quickly as Dr. King had hoped. Three months after King electrified the nation with his dream, President John F. Kennedy, who had championed the civil rights bill, was assassinated. But the dream was not dead. Lyndon Johnson, a Southerner, succeeded Kennedy. He pushed the bill through Congress and signed it into law in 1964. It overrode state statutes, making discrimination in public accommodations illegal. It made school desegregation and voter registration federal matters.

Although it was law, the Civil Rights Act was not always obeyed. So, African Americans continued to fight for justice and equality. This time the battle front was voter registration. In some places in the Deep South, whites used intimidation, poll taxes, and literacy tests to keep blacks from registering to vote.

One of those places was Mississippi. In the "Mississippi Freedom Summer of 1964," seven hundred to nine hundred people, both black and white, descended on the state to help blacks register to vote.[17] Whites responded by bombing or burning thirty-five churches and thirty other buildings, beating at least eighty of the civil rights workers and murdering six.[18]

In the campaign to register African Americans in Selma, Alabama, three thousand people were arrested, including Martin Luther King, Jr. King wanted the nation to see what was happening in the South. So he organized a march from Selma to the state capital in Montgomery, fifty miles away. The march began on March 7, 1965, with six hundred people. They were stopped by state and local police with billy clubs and tear gas. President Johnson sent the Alabama National Guard to protect them and they tried again. On March 21, thirty-two hundred people set out from Selma. Many had come from distant cities. By the time the event ended four days later, twenty-five thousand had joined the march. The protest not only showed the nation what was happening to African Americans in the South, it united them against it.

President Lyndon Johnson referred to the Selma-to-Montgomery march when he asked Congress to pass the Voting Rights Act. Johnson said, "Their cause must be our cause. Because it is not just Negroes, but really it is all of us, who must overcome the crippling legacy of bigotry and injustice. . . . And we shall overcome."[19]

The legacy of bigotry and injustice, rooted in slavery, was still strong in 1965, one hundred years after slavery ended. African Americans had chipped away at that legacy in a hard-fought, bloody battle for their rights. Now they wanted to totally demolish it through another battle—this time for power.

# CHAPTER 6

# EXERCISING POWER: 1966-1972

For the century after emancipation, African Americans had focused their struggle for equality on their rights as American citizens. It had taken a hundred years for people to acknowledge that blacks had just as much right to vote, to go to school, and to ride public transportation as any other citizen. But the mere fact that they had legal rights did not mean that they could enjoy those rights. In many places around the country, whites found ways around the civil rights laws. A rising number of blacks was becoming dissatisfied with rights that existed only on paper. They were convinced that they would never have the same rights as white people without the same power.

In the mid 1960s, younger blacks, especially, were growing impatient with the inch-by-inch struggle for freedoms. One of those most impatient was Stokely Carmichael, a leader of the Student Nonviolent Coordinating Committee (SNCC). This group had been formed when college students led the sit-in movement. It had broken down many walls of prejudice. But it was progressing too slowly for Carmichael. Attacks and arrests during a 1966 march for voting rights in Mississippi angered him. He told the demonstrators that nonviolence was not working. What they needed was not rights, not integration, but power—"Black power!" he yelled.

The crowd went wild with agreement. "What do we want?" Carmichael asked them. "Black power!" they answered. "What do we want?" he called again and again. "Black power!" they chanted over and over.

To Carmichael and several of the other younger blacks who were rising to leadership in the various civil rights organizations, the term "black power" was inviting. It recalled a dignity that had been stifled by centuries of white rule, a pride in being black. It suggested an ability and a control that had been hidden under years of white restrictions. It stirred up a militancy that had been forbidden by the older, more religious civil rights leaders such as King and Abernathy.

Stokely Carmichael's call to black power was not a completely new idea. It was inspired by the speeches of a black nationalist named Malcolm X.

# BLACK IDENTITY

Born in Michigan, Malcolm Little grew up hating white people for reasons that he felt were justified. His father had been murdered by racists and his home burned by the KKK. His anger led him to crime. In prison, he joined the Nation of Islam. The Nation of Islam was a movement begun in the 1930s that taught that blacks were superior to all other groups. As a Black Muslim, Malcolm renounced the name "Little"—the name of a slave master, handed down to his slaves. Instead, he called himself "X." The X symbolized his real identity, which had

Malcolm X advocated the separation of the races in America. The charismatic speaker's message was considered a counter to what Martin Luther King, Jr. preached.

been lost. Malcolm X believed that the true identity of the black man was being lost in his struggle to be accepted in the white community. He preached separation. The majority of blacks, he said, do not want "to live mixed up with the white man." Instead, he argued, they "prefer the company of their own kind."[1] Malcolm X was very popular, especially with African Americans in northern cities. He was a powerful speaker and he expressed their frustrations passionately. Malcolm X urged black Americans to do everything they could to be self-sufficient, and not to depend on white people. He felt that African Americans should build their own neighborhoods, schools, and businesses. They should hire African Americans and shop at African-American stores. They should start social programs to deal with community problems.

And perhaps the most controversial of Malcolm X's ideas: If treated wrongly by whites, they should fight back. He was opposed to violence generally, but believed all people had a right to defend themselves. He reasoned, "It is criminal to teach a man not to defend himself when he is the constant victim of brutal attacks."[2] In this belief, he disagreed with Martin Luther King, Jr.'s advocacy of nonviolence.

Malcolm X became the victim of brutal attacks himself. After disagreements with some in the Nation of Islam, he broke away from the group. Black Muslims bombed his home and then shot and killed him as he was speaking to a large rally in 1965. But his writings and speeches continued to inspire thousands long after his death. Many agreed with him that they would never achieve justice by waiting for whites to give it to them.

# ANGER IN THE CITIES

Many urban blacks lived in broken-down houses owned by whites, next to white-owned businesses that employed only whites. Their schools, their job opportunities, and even the food in their overpriced grocery stores were less than poor. The inner-city slums were much like the slave quarters of the old South—abandoned and exploited by white masters.

In the summers of 1964–1968, the African-American residents of these urban ghettos exercised their black power by revolting. They rose up in desperation over the discrimination that kept them in substandard conditions. Most of the urban riots began with an incident involving a white police officer and a black citizen.

The first was in Harlem in 1964. An off-duty police officer shot and killed a fifteen-year-old African American. Blacks responded by attacking the police, breaking windows in white-owned buildings, and looting white-owned stores. Similar riots occurred in two other areas of New York that summer as well as in at least four other northern cities.

One of the biggest urban riots broke out the next summer in the Watts area of Los Angeles. As with the previous incidents, police action triggered the event. A white police officer arrested a black resident for reckless driving. Witnesses thought the police officer was more forceful with the young man than necessary, and an ugly crowd gathered. The anger raged for six days over forty-six square miles. It took fourteen thousand National Guardsmen to calm it. When it was over, thirty-four people were dead (mostly African Americans, killed by police), 898 were injured, and $45 million of property was destroyed.[3]

The country plunged into despair and chaos after the assassination of Martin Luther King, Jr. Riots and violence erupted in cities across the nation, including these blocks of Washington, D.C.

In the next two summers, police arrests launched riots in more than 150 cities. Buildings were burned, property was stolen, and lives were lost. In Detroit, Michigan, forty-three people were killed. A presidential commission assigned to study the urban unrest concluded that the cause was white racism.

White racism led to one final flurry of devastating riots. On April 4, 1968, a white man, James Earl Ray, shot and killed Martin Luther King, Jr. Immediately, more than one hundred cities erupted in rage. More buildings burned, more looting occurred, and more people were killed. The most vocal champion of nonviolence had been silenced, and the leadership of the struggle for fairness fell to younger, less patient men. The black power movement became more militant.

# DEFIANCE ON DISPLAY

Perhaps the most glaring example of the militancy occurred during the 1968 Summer Olympics. Two African Americans won medals in the 200-meter track and field event: Tommie Smith took the gold and John Carlos took the bronze. When the two men stood on the winners' platform, they wore black scarves around their necks to symbolize their pride in being black. They wore black socks, but they had no shoes—to tell all who were watching that blacks in the United States lived in poverty.

When the American flag was raised and the US anthem began, Smith lifted his black-gloved right fist as a sign of black power. Carlos raised his left fist, also covered with a black glove, to represent black unity. While the music played, they closed their eyes and bowed their heads, not in reverence, but in disdain for the country that was not, as far as they were concerned, "the land of the free."

The country they scorned suspended the two athletes from its team. But the statement had been made. The world had seen the pain and defiance of America's young African Americans.

That pain was also evident in the African-American writers of the time. James Baldwin's novels depicted the suffering and abuse endured by African Americans. Dramatist and poet Amiri Baraka, also known as LeRoi Jones, spoke strongly against white values. Poet Gwendolyn Brooks also described white values and culture as oppressive to blacks.

# ARMED DEFIANCE

One of the most defiant expressions of the black power movement was the Black Panther Party for Self-Defense. It was formed by two young, northern African Americans who were influenced by the ideas of Malcolm X and Marxist (Communist) writers. Huey Newton and Bobby Seale, who had been in numerous skirmishes with the law, created the organization in 1966 to shield African Americans in Oakland, California, from what they considered police harassment. Seale insisted that the only way to protect inner-city African Americans was "by organizing black self-defense groups that are dedicated to defending [the] black community from racist police oppression and brutality."[4]

They called their group "panthers" because panthers do not attack unless backed into a corner, and then they attack viciously. They felt that the police had backed them up against a wall of economic, social, and political injustice. And they intended to respond viciously.

At first, they simply acquired guns legally and followed Oakland police officers, making sure they were not abusing African Americans. They wore black berets and black leather jackets to intimidate and enhance their military appearance.

The confident aggressiveness of the Black Panthers appealed to angry young black men. The group's popularity spread to other cities, and the party may have had as many as five thousand members at one point.

But their popularity waned as nearly all the leaders were accused of serious crimes: drug trafficking, prostitution, assault, and murder. Several were sent to prison; others died in police shoot-outs.

In 1972, Huey Newton, out of jail between charges, completely reformed the Panthers. Instead of advocating armed resistance, the party focused on practical help for the African-American community.

The Black Panther Party's goals were equality, freedom, and fair treatment. Cofounders Bobby Seale, left, and Huey Newton dispatched armed patrols to challenge the practice of police brutality.

It distributed food and shoes to children, provided free medical services, and started a school. The concept of "black power" had become less militant and more service oriented.

> APPROXIMATELY THREE HUNDRED NEGRO MALES AND FEMALES, MANY WEARING BLACK PANTHER BUTTONS AND BERETS, MARCHED TO WINDSOR COMMUNITY CENTER . . . PLAYED A RECORDING OF MALCOLM X SPEECH AND HEARD TWO SPEAKERS. CROWD RAISED FISTS IN BLACK POWER SALUTE NUMEROUS TIMES BUT DISPERSED . . .[5] —from a report by the Federal Bureau of Investigation (FBI)

# QUIET POWER

African-American political power was growing. The Voting Rights Act of 1965 brought more African-American voters to the polls, and the activism of the 1950s and 1960s brought African-American names to the ballot. In 1968, nine African Americans were elected to Congress, including one woman and the first African-American senator since Reconstruction. Two cities had African-American mayors, and some African Americans were elected to both state and local government positions.

The nine new and six sitting African-American congresspeople formed a committee to focus some of their energies on the problems that faced African Americans. In 1971, the committee became known as the Congressional Black Caucus. The Caucus, still going strong in the twenty-first century, has investigated racial incidents, exposed racism, and written legislation furthering equality for all.

Elective office was not the only form of political power for African Americans in the late 1960s and early 1970s. The executive and judicial branches of government also opened up to African Americans. Robert

The thirteen founding members of the Congressional Black Caucus organized in 1971. The caucus, which still exists today, aims to achieve greater equality for African Americans.

Weaver was appointed by President Lyndon Johnson to his cabinet in 1966 as Secretary of the new department of Housing and Urban Development. Thurgood Marshall, who had successfully argued the case of *Brown v. Board of Education* in 1954, became a US Supreme Court justice in 1967.

The National Black Political Convention was held in 1972. This conference was the crowning achievement of the black power movement. It brought together influential blacks of every type. Delegates included disciples of slain civil rights hero Martin Luther King, Jr., such as the preacher and activist Jesse Jackson. Representatives of the fading militant

> What is important is a goal toward which we are moving, a goal that is the basis of true democracy. . . . But you must pray for it and work for it, and that goal is very simple. That goal is that if a child, a Negro child, is born to a black mother in a state like Mississippi or any other state . . . he is born with the exact same rights as a similar child born to a white parent of the wealthiest person in the United States. No, it's not true. It never will be true. But I challenge anybody to take the position that that is not the goal that we should be shooting for. —Thurgood Marshall at age 80 in a speech to the National Bar Association.[6]

movement, such as Black Panther founder Bobby Seale, attended. Radical extremists such as Black Muslim Louis Farrakhan attended. More moderate leaders such as mayors Richard Hatcher and Carl Stokes were part of the gathering.

Convention attendees discussed community health centers, urban improvement, and minimum wage guarantees. Their concerns were not clenched-fist demands for more power, but practical help for the poor of all races. They had stepped over the color line into positions of genuine power. It looked like they had a chance to improve the conditions of African Americans, to reverse the wrongs of the previous 350 years. Would they actually be able to overcome centuries of oppressive acts and prejudicial attitudes? Could they change perceptions of whites and blacks alike about the character, abilities, and potential of all citizens? How long would it take?

# CHAPTER 7

# ARE WE THERE YET?: BEYOND 1972

**B**y the time the National Black Political Convention met in 1972, the United States had come a long way from where it was even ten years earlier. But had the country fulfilled its promise to the children of slavery? Were African Americans where they were should be? Where they were told they would be on the plantations in 1865—"just the same" as white Americans?

If blacks in the United States were "just the same" as their white brothers and sisters, there would be no segregation and no discrimination. The schools black children attend would be either the same schools or exactly like the schools where white children study. African Americans would have the same housing and employment opportunities as all other citizens. Are we there yet?

# TWO TYPES OF SEGREGATION

The civil rights and black power movements brought an end to *de jure* segregation—separation that was legal. According to law—the Fourteenth Amendment; the Civil Rights Acts of 1964, 1965, 1968, 1988, and 1991; and other federal and state legislation—African Americans are entitled to every right and privilege white Americans can claim. But despite what laws say, *de facto* segregation has remained a reality in many places. De facto segregation is separation that occurs as a result of where people live and what resources are available to them.

De facto segregation has been one of the longest-lived legacies of slavery. For decades after emancipation, most of the freedmen could not find good-paying jobs. Therefore, they remained poor. The schools in their impoverished neighborhoods could not attract good teachers or afford enriching experiences, so the education they provided was substandard. Besides, many poor blacks had to leave school early to make what money they could to add to the family income. With low academic skills, they could not get jobs that would pay them enough to move out of their situation. The great majority of blacks remained in poverty— while whites moved out of the poorer neighborhoods. Thus for many decades, in schools, businesses, and neighborhoods throughout the land, the two races were separate and unequal.

De facto segregation was a cycle that was difficult to escape. Very few people could lift themselves out of it without help. After passage of the Civil Rights Acts of the 1960s, a number of leaders realized they had a responsibility to do something to correct the injustices of decades. To reverse the wrongs of the past they had to break the cycle of de facto segregation in three places: education, housing, and employment.

# EDUCATION

Segregation existed in education because children went to schools in the neighborhoods in which they lived. In one county in North Carolina, officials decided the way to mix students was to move some to new

Court-ordered busing policies in the 1970s ignited racial hostilities in several US cities. This photo shows a fight that erupted among students protesting the busing laws in Boston in 1976.

neighborhoods for their education. A court ordered that the county's 107 public schools be integrated by busing. Some inner-city children were bused to suburban schools and some suburban children were bused to inner-city schools. When the order survived a court challenge, other courts demanded that districts use busing to desegregate their schools.[1]

Many people, both black and white, protested. They wanted their children to attend schools near their homes. The debate over court-ordered busing was one of the biggest controversies of the 1970s. Some districts imposed the court mandate and others balked. Some instituted voluntary busing. They put attractive specialty programs in predominately black schools and bused white children who wanted to attend those "magnet" programs to the inner-city schools. Some districts allowed African-American and other minority students who wanted to go to schools out of their neighborhoods to transfer to those schools. The districts that refused outright to implement some form of busing lost federal funding.

The busing policy lost most of its teeth with two Supreme Court decisions in 1973 and 1974. The court ruled that it was fair for richer school districts to spend more money on students than poor districts because the "right" to an education was not guaranteed in the Constitution.[2] The court also said that a school district could draw its boundaries wherever it wanted, which permitted *de facto* segregation to continue in education.[3]

The limited success in desegregating public schools led Milwaukee, Wisconsin, to look for a way black students could attend predominately white private schools. The private institutions generally offered a better education than the public schools in the poor neighborhoods, but low-income parents could not afford the tuition the private schools charged. The solution was simple: give parents the money the public school would spend educating their children—in a coupon called a voucher—and let the parents spend the money at the private school of their choice. Vouchers would be available only to families that fell below a certain income limit, and they might cover all or only part of the tuition, depending on the school the parents chose.

Milwaukee began the voucher program in 1990 with three hundred children in seven schools. The program was so popular it was expanded statewide and in the 2014–2015 school year served 29,683 students in two hundred schools.[4] Wisconsin's school voucher program launched a school-choice movement that spread throughout the country. The movement includes other choices, mainly choices among various forms of public education such as charter schools and permission to enroll in any public school.

Using choice as a means to desegregate education has come with a few problems. Some of the public school choice programs have led to re-segregation; several charter schools, for example, have become neighborhood schools of all one ethnicity. Programs that open private schools to students are more successful, but voucher programs are not widely available. In 2015 only six states offered vouchers to students on the basis of income.[5] Another problem is that parents can exercise their choice only if they have the transportation and the time to get their children to and from the school they select. Those resources are usually restricted by inequalities in housing.

Where are we today with educational equality? We are further along than before the *Brown v. Board of Education* decision of 1954, but—almost unbelievably—no further than in 1968. Although some strides were made in the 1970s and 1980s, a series of legal actions and court rulings from 1991 to 2007 reversed much of the progress. In the *Board of Education of Oklahoma City Public Schools v. Dowell* decision, the Supreme Court relieved school districts of requirements to desegregate their schools. The judges declared that federal orders for schools to integrate had always "been intended as temporary measures to remedy past discrimination."[6] Schools that had once complied with the federal orders did not have to be concerned with integration any longer. The ruling, together with others, let public school districts completely ignore the racial make-up of their classrooms.

Without intentional efforts to maintain equality, public schools throughout the country reverted to segregation. The proportion of black students in substantially integrated schools dropped to 23.3 percent in 2011, below the figure for 1968.[7] Re-segregation, and thus inequality in education, is likely to remain a trend as long as inequity continues in housing.

Racist whites made it known that African Americans were not welcome to live in their neighborhoods. As blacks began to move into white suburbs, fears arose that property values would decline.

# HOUSING

As in education, blacks and whites had equal access to housing opportunities under the law since the 1960s. But again as in education, people who did not want black families in their neighborhoods found ways around the law. They raised prices so high African Americans could not afford to purchase homes. Mortgage companies drew red lines on maps around areas where blacks lived and refused to do business in those areas, claiming the neighborhoods were too risky.

Meanwhile, as American jobs shifted away from a dependence on manufacturing, people did not need to live in the hearts of cities to find work. Many white people, especially, began relocating to the higher-priced suburbs in the 1970s. This movement, sometimes called "white flight," left inner areas of cities to those who could not afford to leave. Many inner cities became African-Americans ghettos, abandoned by businesses and neglected by government.

The Fair Housing Act of 1968 put an end to much of the obvious discrimination. But the legislation has not improved the inner cities. Nor has it helped African Americans find housing in better neighborhoods.

Americans have known that one's status of birth is not a permanent condition. Americans believed that you might not control your circumstances but you can control your response. And your greatest ally in controlling your response to your circumstances has been a quality education. But today, when I can look at your zip code and I can tell whether you're going to get a good education, can I honestly say it does not matter where you came from, it matters where you are going? The crisis in K-12 education is a threat to the very fabric of who we are. . . . We need to give parents greater choice, particularly poor parents whose kids, very often minorities, are trapped in failing neighborhood schools. This is the civil rights issue of our day.

—Condeleezza Rice, 66th US Secretary of State, in a speech at the Republican National Convention, August 29, 2012.[8]

Decades after blacks were told they were "just the same" as whites, the difference between them in home ownership is still stark. In 2014, fewer than 44 percent of black householders owned their homes whereas 73 percent of white householders owned theirs.[9] However, the issue is not really fairness in housing; it is fairness in employment.

# EMPLOYMENT

If African Americans could get good jobs, they could choose where they lived and thus where their children went to school. But years of racism and poor schools had kept blacks on the lowest levels of the workforce. So when discrimination in hiring was forbidden legally and African Americans could compete for jobs, they entered the race at a disadvantage. They qualified only for the lowest-paying positions. Presidents Kennedy and Johnson recognized that the only way most grandchildren of slavery would have a chance at a decent job would be if they were given a little edge. That edge became known as affirmative action.

The first mention of affirmative action came in an executive order issued by President John Kennedy in 1961. Kennedy's order required that all companies that used any government money "take affirmative action to ensure that applicants"—specifically minority applicants—were employed and treated fairly.[10]

Kennedy did not say what "taking affirmative action" meant. But his successor, Lyndon Johnson, explained what it meant and how it would help to right the wrongs of slavery:

> You do not wipe away the scars of centuries by saying: Now you are free to go where you want, and do as you desire. . . . You do not take a person, who for years, has been hobbled by chains and liberate him, bring him up to the starting line of a race and then say, "you are free to compete with all the others," and still justly believe that you have been completely fair. . . . We seek not just freedom but opportunity.[11]

> Affirmative action is a recognition that there is a history of negative action, restraint of trade, restraint of opportunities based upon gender, and based upon race. . . . when allowed to work it has opened up doors. By inclusion it has expanded our economy. We now have more women, more people of color, who are consumers, producers, part of an educated work-force, lawyers, doctors, socially-useful public servants.[12]—Reverend Jesse Jackson

By the time President Johnson issued Executive Order 11246 in 1965, which reaffirmed the concept, employers understood that "taking affirmative action" meant doing something intentional to see that African Americans were recruited, hired, and promoted.

As with the ambiguous mandate of "all deliberate speed" ten years earlier, the term "affirmative action" was fuzzy enough that it could not be enforced. So President Richard Nixon made the order clearer. In October 1969, he ordered all the construction unions in Philadelphia that had government contracts to implement a plan for hiring minorities.[13] The unions had to conduct a census of the city to determine what percentage of the population was African American, Asian, American Indian, and Hispanic. Then they had to hire people so their workforce contained the same percentages. The Philadelphia order defined affirmative action as quotas for each minority group.

Affirmative action began as a mandate only for the federal government in hiring for government jobs. In the 1970s, the practice was extended beyond federal jobs to companies, unions, and universities across America. The hope was that giving African Americans and members of other minority groups extra preference would enable them to "catch up" to the rest of the population; eventually it would no longer be needed.

After fifty years, has affirmative action—or any other measure—achieved the goal of equalizing employment opportunities? Some say

The *Bakke* Supreme Court decision was protested by affirmative action supporters in 1978. Affirmative action continues to be a controversial issue among Americans.

the country still has a long way to go. They point to the fact that the overwhelming majority of high-paying jobs are not held by African Americans: 96 percent of CEOs, 86 percent of partners in law firms, and 85 percent of college professors are white men.[14] Other economic statistics reveal a wide gap between the races. African Americans earn less than 60 percent of what whites earn and the jobless rate for African Americans is more than twice the rate for whites. One in ten whites and one in four blacks live in poverty.[15]

# AFFIRMATIVE ACTION IN HIGHER EDUCATION

Perhaps the greatest success of affirmative action has not come in employment, but in education. When affirmative action began, and especially when it expanded to include college enrollment, many people accepted and even welcomed it as a short-term remedy to the unfairness of the past. It was an extra boost for African Americans to make up for years of subjection. But as time passed and the policy remained, some white Americans began to criticize affirmative action as reverse discrimination—discrimination against nonblacks.

In 1977, one man brought his complaint to the Supreme Court. For two years, Allan Bakke was denied admission to medical school. The school admitted one hundred applicants a year, but sixteen of them had to be minority. Bakke's test scores were considerably higher than those of some of the minority applicants who got in to the program. Bakke protested that his Fourteenth Amendment rights were violated—he had been denied admission on the basis of his white race. The court ruled that rigid quotas could not be imposed but affirmative action was not illegal.[16] In other words, the school could not hold a certain number of places open for minorities, but it could take other steps to help minorities get in.

The Bakke ruling was a little unclear. So in 1995, President Bill Clinton issued guidelines for affirmative action programs: No action should create a quota, give preferences to people who are not qualified, or discriminate in reverse. And a company or school should stop practicing affirmative action when "its equal opportunity purposes have been achieved." Clinton believed that affirmative action was a good policy as long as discrimination exists.[17]

Discrimination still existed in 2003, when the Supreme Court heard two affirmative action cases. The University of Michigan gave preference to minority applicants in both its undergraduate program and its law school. The law school recruited and admitted minorities so it would have a racially diverse group of students. The undergraduate program achieved diversity by giving extra points to minority applicants. President George W. Bush believed both policies were unconstitutional.

The court's ruling was mixed. The justices said the undergraduate program's policy was unconstitutional because its point system, like quotas, was unfair. The law school's admission process, however, was ruled acceptable. As in the Bakke case, quotas were not allowed, but the general principle of affirmative action was upheld.

People continue to debate the value of affirmative action in higher education. Some, including a number of African Americans, say minorities no longer need or want the extra help. Other people point out that the unending cycle of poor neighborhoods, poor schools, and poor job opportunities still place minorities at a disadvantage. Affirmative action, they believe, is needed to overcome that disadvantage.

# CULTURAL PRIDE

African-American disadvantage in the 1970s was more than education-al and economic. It was cultural. Despite the richness of their culture, most African Americans did not know their heritage. The history books their children studied did not mention Revolutionary War hero Peter Salem, pioneer James Beckwourth, or gunboat captain Robert Smalls. They did not show pictures of the African-American "buffalo soldiers" who helped open the west. English classes did not study the writings of William Wells Brown, Ralph Ellison, or Lorraine Hansberry. Neither blacks nor whites knew the contributions African Americans had made to their country.

That began to change in the late 1960s. Young African Americans who had managed to get into universities were feeling the racial pride that was part of the black power movement. They looked for courses that addressed their heritage. Students demanded that colleges offer classes in the history and culture of African Americans. And they wanted those classes to be taught by African-American professors.

Now many universities have departments or programs of African-American Studies. The original purpose of these studies, according to the College of William and Mary, was to correct "the omissions and distortions of mainstream American education."[18]

# CELEBRATING AFRICAN AMERICANS

Omitting the achievements of African Americans was one of the legacies of slavery. Black Americans fought in every one of America's wars, made important scientific discoveries, excelled in the arts, surpassed most others in sports, and made significant contributions to American culture at every stage of history. Yet knowledge of those accomplishments was lost in a world of white domination. In an attempt to right the wrongs of omission, Americans have recognized and now celebrate some of the successes of black Americans.

One long-forgotten success took place on the baseball field. Before Jackie Robinson broke the color barrier, African-American athletes were performing great feats in their own league. One of the fastest pitchers of all time, Satchel Paige, was not selected for the Baseball Hall of Fame until 1971, nineteen years after playing in an all-star game. A year later, Josh Gibson and Buck Leonard—great players but unknown because they played on African-American teams—were also belatedly elected to the Baseball Hall of Fame.

African Americans have celebrated their own achievements since Carter G. Woodson, the son of a former slave, established Black History Week in 1926. In 1976, as part of the celebration of America's

The election of the United States' first African-American president, Barack Obama, in 2007 carried with it tremendous historical importance.

bicentennial, the event was expanded to a month. Today the entire nation observes February as Black History Month. Schoolchildren and others set aside that month to learn and applaud the history and culture of African Americans.

Another form of recognition took thirty years. In 1968, four days after Martin Luther King, Jr., was assassinated, a congressperson suggested having a national holiday to celebrate his life and work. He reasoned that King was a hero not just to African Americans, but to all freedom-loving Americans. People debated the proposal. Some states set aside a day to honor the civil rights leader, but in 1986 a legal holiday was declared. President Ronald Reagan named the third Monday in January a day to remember King. Still, it was not celebrated in all fifty states until 1999.[19]

With every year that goes by, America has more African-American achievements to celebrate. Black people have enriched the country in every field. Four Nobel laureates, more than forty-five Pulitzer Prize recipients and over forty Academy Award winners or nominees have been African American. Black Americans have distinguished themselves in sports, science, law, medicine, education, business, and politics. In 1983 Guion S. Bluford, Jr., became the first African-American astronaut, and in 2008 Barack Obama was elected the first black president of the United States.

# RIGHTING THE WRONGS

Although these achievements demonstrate progress, the nation remained plagued for some time by the memory of injustices that remained unsettled. One of the insults of slavery and its aftermath that angered blacks the most was the fact that white people were not punished for blatant and cruel crimes against blacks. This was one of the wrongs that was righted—to a limited extent—after the civil rights and black power movements. In the 1990s, the FBI opened some long-abandoned cases.

The murderer of Medgar Evers, Byron De La Beckwith, had been set free by white juries that deadlocked in two trials in 1964. Because he was not acquitted, he could be tried again. Thirty years later, when he was seventy-three years old, he was convicted and sentenced to life in prison. Justice was late, but it was done.

Justice was forty years overdue for Edgar Ray Killeen. He was one of a group of men who beat and shot three civil rights workers in Mississippi in 1964. The incident attracted national attention because two of the workers were white. Eighteen Klansmen were arrested, but none was charged with murder. Seven were convicted of violating civil rights laws, but the longest sentence any of them served was six years. Outraged after seeing the 1988 movie *Mississippi Burning* describing the crime, a reporter hunted down the murderers, who were still living. In 2005 Edgar Ray Killeen, age seventy-nine, was finally found guilty of manslaughter and sentenced to sixty years in the Mississippi State Penitentiary. Representative John Lewis said after the trial, "It is never, ever too late to bring about justice."[20]

Justice was also served late but decisively on the people who killed African-American children in a 1963 Sunday school bombing. The four Klansman who committed the crime had been identified as suspects within weeks, but none was even brought to trial until 1977. At that time, one suspect was tried and convicted. The second died in 1994. The third and fourth were convicted in 2001 and 2002. They were sentenced to life in prison. "The time for justice is here," the prosecutor told the jury. "It's way overdue."[21]

# SOCIAL JUSTICE: THE NEW CIVIL RIGHTS MOVEMENT

If justice was "way overdue" in 2002, some people believe it is still too long in coming. They see disparities between blacks and whites widening rather than narrowing. White households had thirteen times more wealth than black households in 2013; this gap is the biggest in thirty years of keeping records.[22] On every measure of health and success, African Americans fall below white Americans. In addition to the glaring economic and educational inequalities, blacks have higher rates of incarceration, teen birth, and infant mortality.

Perhaps more troubling than the statistics are the experiences and perceptions of African Americans regarding unequal treatment. A 2013 Pew Research study found that two thirds of black people surveyed thought courts were unfair to African Americans and seven out of ten believed the police treated them unjustly. A little over a third said they had personally experienced racial discrimination in the year of the study. Most telling of all, 91 percent said more needs to be done to achieve racial equality—79 percent said "a lot more" needs to happen before black Americans are "just the same" as whites.[23]

The fact that these perceptions and the realities that underlie them have persisted for so many decades has led to the twenty-first-century movement of social justice. The movement is an attempt to create a just society—a world in which all people are treated fairly. People have different understandings of what makes a society just. Some see social justice as equal treatment and equal opportunity; others see it as equal share of all a community's resources.

The different definitions mean that people who want social justice have different goals. Some want only to change discriminatory laws, stop unequal enforcement of laws, and remove barriers that keep people from achieving all they are capable of. Others want to redistribute wealth more evenly.

The social justice movement is in many ways a new civil rights movement. It has expanded the notion of a civil right beyond political rights to include social and economic "rights." Some claim a right to a specific wage, quality healthcare, and a college education, for example. The movement has embraced the causes of groups other than African Americans, including other ethnic groups, the disabled, the elderly, and immigrants.

As with the Black Power movement of the 1960s, the modern push for social justice is seen mostly in young people. Many of the older organizations such as the NAACP and the National Urban League are still working to bring about racial equality, but the energy is with the young activists. Using electronic and social media, they respond almost immediately to incidents of perceived injustice. They organize large events that disrupt complacent communities, calling attention to problems and demanding change.

Will this modern civil rights phenomenon be any more successful than the movements of the past? Men and women of previous eras were able to get just laws passed, strike down discriminatory practices, and create opportunities where they did not exist. But prejudicial attitudes have not been entirely erased. In some ways the nation has slipped back into segregated thinking and acting. And new groups are presenting fresh social justice pressures. Today's challenge is the same as yesterday's: ensuring that every American is "just the same" as every other American. We aren't quite there yet.

# TIMELINE

**1863**   **January 1**: Emancipation Proclamation signed by Abraham Lincoln, declaring slaves in the areas of rebellion free.

**1865**   **March 3**: Freedmen's Bureau established to help former slaves transition to freedom.

**1865**   **April 9**: Civil War ended.

**1865**   **December 18**: Thirteenth Amendment was ratified and became law, forbidding slavery anywhere in the United States.

**1865–1866**   Southern states enacted Black Codes.

**1866**   **April 9**: Congress passed Civil Rights Act of 1866 over presidential veto.

**1867**   Ku Klux Klan officially organized.

**1868**   **July 21**: Fourteenth Amendment was ratified and became law.

**1870**   **March 30**: Fifteenth Amendment was ratified and became law.

**1896**   **May 18**: In *Plessy v. Ferguson*, the Supreme Court upheld the principle of "separate but equal."

**1915**   Ku Klux Klan revived.

**1919** Violent racial clashes gave this year's summer the name "Red Summer."

**1941** **June 21**: President Franklin Roosevelt issued Executive Order 8802, outlawing discrimination in defense industries.

**1948** President Harry Truman issued Executive Order 9981, prohibiting discrimination in the armed forces.

**1954** **May 17**: In *Brown v. Board of Education*, Supreme Court ruled segregation unconstitutional.

**1955–1956** Montgomery, Alabama, bus boycott ended some forms of segregation.

**1957** **September 4**: Arkansas Governor Orval Faubus used the National Guard to prevent nine black students from enrolling in Little Rock's Central High School.

**1960** **February 1**: First sit-in held, in Greensboro, North Carolina.

**1960** Freedom Riders beaten in Alabama.

**1963** **April 3**: Birmingham demonstrations began.

**1963** **August 28**: At March on Washington, Martin Luther King, Jr., delivered "I Have a Dream" speech.

**1964** **March 25**: Selma to Montgomery march ended.

**1964** **July**: Civil Rights Act enacted.

**1965** **August**: Voting Rights Act passed.

**1965–1968** Riots occurred in Watts, California; Newark, New Jersey; Detroit, Michigan; and other cities.

**1966** October 15: Black Panther Party formed in Oakland, California.

**1972** March 10–12: National Black Political Convention held in Gary, Indiana.

**2008** Barack Obama became first African American elected to the US presidency.

# CHAPTER NOTES

## INTRODUCTION

1. T. Lindsay Baker and Julie P. Baker, eds., "Katie Rowe," *The WPA Oklahoma Slave Narratives* (Norman: University of Oklahoma, 1996), pp. 364–371; Hatie Rowe, "Oklahoma Slave Narrative," *A Little History*, n.d., http://freepages.genealogy.rootsweb.com/~ewyatt/_borders Oklahoma%2 Slave%20Narratives/ Rowe,%20Hatie.html (January 6, 2004).
2. Ibid.
3. Ibid.
4. Alan Brinkley, *American History: A Survey*, 9th edition (New York: McGraw-Hill, 1995), vol. l: To 1877, p. 70.
5. Ibid., p. 310.
6. T. Lindsay Baker and Julie P. Baker, eds., "Mrs. Isabella Jackson," *The WPA Oklahoma Slave Narratives* (Norman: University of Oklahoma, 1996), p. 216.

## CHAPTER 1. REALLY FREE? 1865–1866

1. Fountain Hughes, "Personal Narrative," *Slavery and the Making of America*, http://www.pbs.org/wnet/slavery/experience/freedom/narratives.html (accessed November 17, 2015).
2. "Political Affairs," *The New York Times*, October 7, 1866, p. 2.
3. George W. Cable, "The Freedman's Case in Equity," *Century Magazine*, February 1884, pp. 408–418.
4. Joel Chandler Harris, *Joel Chandler Harris' Life of Henry W. Grady: Including His Writings and Speeches* (New York: Cassell, 1890), p. 100.
5. George T. Winston, "The Relationship of the Whites to the Negroes," *Annals of the American Academy of Political and Social Science*, vol. 18, July 1901, pp. 105–118.

6. Benjamin M. Boyer, Congressional Globe, 39th Congress, 1st session, January 10, 1866, pp. 100–101.
7. William Parker, "The Freedman's Story: In Two Parts," *Documenting the American South*, 1999, http://docsouth.unc.edu/parker/parker.html (February 3, 2004).
8. George K. Holmes, "The Peons of the South," *Annals of the American Academy of Political and Social Science*, vol. 4, September 1893, p. 67.
9. R. Jackson Wilson, James Gilbert, Karen Ordahl Kupperman, Stephen Nissenbaum, and Donald M. Scott, eds., *The Pursuit of Liberty: A History of the American People*, 3rd ed. (New York: HarperCollins, 1996), vol. 2: Since 1865, p. 20.

# CHAPTER 2. FREEDOM IS NOT EQUALITY: 1865–1877

1. R. Jackson Wilson, James Gilbert, Karen Ordahl Kupperman, Stephen Nissenbaum, and Donald M. Scott, eds., *The Pursuit of Liberty: A History of the American People*, 3rd ed. (New York: HarperCollins, 1996), vol. 2: Since 1865, p. 31.
2. "Black Codes of Mississippi," *Afro-American Almanac*, n.d., http://www.toptags.com/aama/docs/bcodes.htm (February 4, 2004).
3. Harvey Wish, ed., *Reconstruction in the South, 1865–1877: Firsthand Accounts of the American Southland After the Civil War, by Southerners and Northerners* (New York: Farrar, Straus, and Giroux, 1965), p. 14.
4. Kenneth M. Stampp, *The Era of Reconstruction, 1865–1877* (New York: Alfred A. Knopf, 1965), p. 136.
5. Ibid., p. 200.
6. Ibid., p. 132.
7. Alan Brinkley, *American History: A Survey*, 9th ed. (New York: McGraw-Hill, 1995), vol. II: Since 1865, p. 423.
8. Oliver O. Howard, *Autobiography of Oliver Otis Howard* (New York: The Baker & Taylor Company, 1907), vol. II, p. 390.

# CHAPTER 3. SEPARATE IS NOT EQUAL: 1877–1915

1. "Goals," *The Civil Rights Movement*, http://www.people.virginia. edu/~ptg3r/345/goals/voterights.html.

2. R. Jackson Wilson, James Gilbert, Karen Ordahl Kupperman, Stephen Nissenbaum, and Donald M. Scott, eds., *The Pursuit of Liberty: A History of the American People*, 3rd ed. (New York: HarperCollins, 1996), vol. 2: Since 1865, p. 76.

3. "A Word of Warning, A Former Slave Urges Constitutional Caution," *History Matters*, n.d., http://historymatters.gmu.edu/d/5468/ (February 4, 2004).

4. Martin Luther King, Jr. National Historic Site, "Jim Crow Laws," December 5, 1998, http://www.nps.gov/malu/ documents/jim_crow_laws.htm.

5. *Cumming v. Board of Education of Richmond County*, 175 U.S. 528 (1899).

6. James Oliver Horton and Lois E. Horton, *Hard Road to Freedom: The Story of African America* (New Brunswick, NJ: Rutgers University Press, 2001), p. 206.

7. Richard M. Perloff, "The Press and Lynchings of African Americans," *Journal of Black Studies*, January 2000, p. 315.

8. Booker T. Washington, "Speech at the Atlanta Cotton States and International Exposition," October 18, 1895, http://teachingamerican-history.org/library/index. asp.?documentprint=69 (January 7, 2004).

9. Ibid.

10. John Hope Franklin and Alfred A. Moss, Jr., *From Slavery to Freedom: A History of African Americans*, 8th ed. (New York: McGraw-Hill, 2000), p. 321.

11. Dunbar, Paul Laurence. "Sympathy." Retrieved from Poetry Foundation website, http://www.poetryfoundation.org/poem/175756 (accessed November 17, 2015).

# CHAPTER 4. ACCOMPLISHMENT IS NOT EQUALITY: 1915–1941

1. E. Marvin Goodwin, *Black Migration in America From 1915 to 1960: An Uneasy Exodus* (Wales: Edwin Mellen Press, 1990).

2. James A. Banks and Cherry A. Banks, *March Toward Freedom: A History of Black Americans*, 2nd ed. (Belmont, CA: Fearon-Pitman, 1978), p. 76.

3. James Oliver Horton and Lois E. Horton, *Hard Road to Freedom: The Story of African America* (New Brunswick, NJ: Rutgers University Press, 2001), p. 221.

4. Banks and Banks, p. 77.

5. Lerone Bennett, Jr., *Before the Mayflower: A History of Black America*, 6th ed. (New York: Penguin, 1993), p. 349.

6. Horton and Horton, p. 222.

7. Emmet J. Scott in *Scott's Official History of the Negro in the World War,* 1919, Chapter XIII.

8. Tom Tiede, *American Tapestry: Eyewitness Accounts of the Twentieth Century* (New York: Pharos Books, 1988), p. 29.

9. Marcus Garvey, "Aims and Objects of Movement for Solution of Negro Problem," *Philosophy and Opinions of Marcus Garvey*, Amy Jacques-Garvey, ed., vol. II (Dover, MA: The Majority Press, 1986), p. 38.

10. Marcus Garvey, "The Negro's Greatest Enemy," The Marcus Garvey and UNIA Papers Project, © 1995, http://www.isop.ucla.edu/mgpp/sample01.htm (February 4, 2004).

11. E. David Cronon, Black Moses: *The Story of Marcus Garvey and the Universal Negro Improvement Association* (Madison: University of Wisconsin, 1969), p. 70.

12. Claude McKay, "If We Must Die," *Dark Symphony: Negro Literature in America*, James A. Emanuel and Theodore L. Gross, eds. (New York: Free Press, 1968), p. 94.

13. Horton and Horton, p. 236.

# CHAPTER 5. GAINING GROUND: 1941–1965

1. John Hardman, "The Great Depression and the New Deal," *Edge*, 1999, https://web.stanford.edu/class/e297c/poverty_prejudice/soc_sec/hgreat.htm (accessed November 17, 2015).

2. *Executive Order 8802: Prohibition of Discrimination in the Defense Industry*, June 25, 1941, http://docs.fdrlibrary.marist.edu/od8802t.html (accessed December 2, 2015).

3. James A. Banks and Cherry A. Banks, *March Toward Freedom: A History of Black Americans,* 2nd ed. (Belmont, CA: Fearon-Pitman, 1978), p. 101.

4. Doris Kearns Goodwin, *No Ordinary Time: Franklin and Eleanor Roosevelt: The Home Front in World War II* (New York: Simon and Schuster, 2013, pp. 246-247).

5. James Oliver Horton and Lois E. Horton, *Hard Road to Freedom: The Story of African America* (New Brunswick, N.J.: Rutgers University Press, 2001), p. 233.

6. Jackie Robinson, "Letter From Jackie Robinson to President Eisenhower," *The University of Texas*, n.d., http://www.eisenhower.utexas.edu/dl/LittleRock/RobinsontoDDEMay1358.pdf (February 4, 2004).

7. *Brown v. Board of Education*, 347 U.S. 483 (1954) (USSC+), http://www.nationalcenter.org/brown.html (January 7, 2003).

8. Henry Hampton and Steve Fayer, *Voices of Freedom: An Oral History of the Civil Rights Movement from the 1950s Through the 1980s* (New York: Bantam Books, 1990), pp. 49–50, 51–52.

9. Banks and Banks, p. 112.

10. Hampton and Fayer, p. 6.

11. "Dexter Avenue Baptist Church," *We Shall Overcome: Historic Places of the Civil Rights Movement*, National Park Service, http://www.cr.nps.gov/nr/travel/civilrights/al7.htm.

12. Banks and Banks, p. 117.

13. "F. W. Woolworth Building," *We Shall Overcome: Historic Places of the Civil Rights Movement, National Park Service*, http://www.cr.nps.gov/nr/travel/civilrights/nc1.htm.

14. Martin Luther King, Jr., "Letter from the Birmingham Jail," *Why We Can't Wait* (New York: Harper and Row, 1964), p. 79.

15. Ibid.

16. Martin Luther King, Jr., address at the March on Washington, 1963, *SCLC Newsletter*, vol. 1, no. 12, September 1963, pp. 5, 8.

17. Doug McAdam, *Freedom Summer* (New York: Oxford University Press, 1988), p. 108.

18. Peter M. Bergman and Mort N. Bergman, *The Chronological History of the Negro in America* (New York: New American Library, 1969), p. 587.

19. Banks and Banks, p. 133.

# CHAPTER 6. EXERCISING POWER: 1966–1972

1. Arnold Adoff, ed., *Black on Black: Commentaries by Negro Americans* (New York: The Macmillan Company, 1968), p. 155.

2. "Quotes by Malcolm X," *Official Web Site of Malcolm X,* n.d., http://www.cmgwww.com/historic/malcolm/about/quotes_by.htm (December 11, 2003).

3. Harry S. Ashmore, *Civil Rights and Wrongs: A Memoir of Race and Politics 1944–1994* (New York: Pantheon, 1994), pp. 191–192.

4. Bobby Seale, *Seize the Time* (New York: Random House, 1970), pp. 66–67.

5. "Black Panther Party, North Carolina, Part 1 of 15, Bufile Number: 105-165706," *Federal Bureau of Investigation: Freedom of Information Act*, n.d., http://foia.fbi.gov/bpanther/bpanther1.pdf (February 4, 2004).

6. Stuart Taylor, Jr. and David Binder, "Marshall on Racism," *New York Times*, August 11, 1988, http://www.nytimes.com/1988/08/11/us/washington-talk-briefing-marshall-on-racism.html?_r=0.

# CHAPTER 7. ARE WE THERE YET?: BEYOND 1972

1. "*Swann v. Charlotte-Mecklenburg County Board of Education*, 402 U.S. 1 (1971)," Touro College Jacob D. Fuchsberg Law Center, © 1997, http://www.tourolaw.edu/ patch/Swann (January 7, 2004).
2. "*San Antonio Independent School District v. Rodriguez*, 411 U.S. 1 (1973)," Human & Constitutional Rights, n.d., http://www.hrcr.org/safrica/ equality/san_antonio_rodriguez.html (January 7, 2004).
3. "*Milliken v. Bradley*, 418 U.S. 717 (1974)," *Brown@50:Fulfilling the Promise*, © 2003, http://www.brown@50.org/Browncases/milliken-bradleyI1974.text (January 7, 2004).
4. "History of the School Choice Program, *School Choice Wisconsin*, n.d., http://www.chooseyourschoolwi.org/about-scw/history-of-the-choice-program.html (accessed December 2, 2015).
5. "School Voucher Laws: State-By-State Comparison," *National Conference of State Legislatures*, n.d., http://www.ncsl.org/research/education/voucher-law-comparison.aspx (accessed December 2, 2015).
6. "Board of Education of Oklahoma City Public Schools v. Dowell." *Oyez*. Chicago-Kent College of Law at Illinois Tech, n.d., https://www.oyez.org/cases/1990/89-1080 (accessed December 7, 2015).
7. Tammy Luhby, "5 Disturbing Stats on Black-White Inequality," *CNN Money*, August 21, 2014, http://money.cnn.com/2014/08/21/news/economy/black-white-inequality/ (accessed December 7, 2015).
8. "Condeleezza Rice on Education," *On the Issues*, n.d., http://www.ontheissues.org/Celeb/Condoleezza_Ricc_Education.htm (acccssed December 8, 2015).
9. Gary Orfield and Erica Frankenberg, "Brown at 60: Great Progress, a Long Retreat and an Uncertain Future," *Civil Rights Project*, May 2015, http://civilrightsproject.ucla.edu/research/k-12-education/integration-and-diversity/brown-at-60-great-progress-a-long-retreat-and-an-uncertain-future/Brown-at-60-051814.pdf (accessed December 8, 2015).

10. "Executive Order 10925, March 6, 1961," *University of Michigan Documents Center*, n.d., http://www.lib.umich.edu/govdocs/jfkeo/eo/10925.htm (January 7, 2004).

11. Lyndon Johnson, "President Lyndon B. Johnson's Commencement Address at Howard University," *Lyndon Baines Johnson Library and Museum*, June 4, 1965, http://www.lbjlib.utexas.edu/johnson/archives.hom/speeches.hom/650604.asp. (January 7, 2004).

12. "Interview with Rev. Jesse Jackson," *In Motion Magazine*, March 8, 1998, http://www.inmotionmagazine.com/jjinter.html (April 30, 2004).

13. James T. Patterson, *Grand Expectations*: *The United States, 1945–1974* (New York: Oxford University Press, 1996), pp. 642, 723.

14. Americans for a Fair Chance, "Opportunity Through Affirmative Action," n.d., http://www.civilrights.org/equal-opportunity/factsheets/fact_sheet_packet.pdf (accessed December 7, 2015).

15. Luhby.

16. "*Regents of the University of California v. Bakke*, 438 US265 (1978)," Find Law, n.d., http://caselaw.lp.findlaw. com/scripts/getcase. pl?court=US&vol=438&invoc=265 (January 7, 2004).

17. "Appendix A," *National Archives and Records Administration*, n.d., http://clinton2.nara.gov/WH/EOP/OP/html/aa/ap-a.html (January 7, 2004).

18. College of William and Mary, *Black Studies*, January 19, 2003, http//:www.wm.edu/Black_Studies/index.php.

19. "The Origin of MLK Day, January 15," n.d., http:// creativefolk. com/blackhistory/blackhistory.html#mlk (January 7, 2004).

20. Donna M. Thornton, "Finding Justice, 40 Years Later," *Gadsden Times,* January 10, 2005, https://news.google.com/newspapers?nid=1891&dat=20050110&id=6g8vAAAAIBAJ&sjid=kNwFAAAAIBAJ&pg=1838,844373&hl=en (accessed December 8, 2015).

21. "Jurors Hear of 'Pure Hate' and Then Get Ex-KKK Case," *Associated Press*, May 21, 2002.

22. Rakesh Kochhar and Richard Fry, "Wealth Inequality Has Wid-

ened Along Racial, Ethnic Lines Since End of Great Recession," *Pew Research Center*, December 12, 2014, http://www.pewresearch. org/fact-tank/2014/12/12/racial-wealth-gaps-great-recession/http:// www.pewresearch.org/fact-tank/2014/12/12/racial-wealth-gaps- great-recession/ (accessed December 9, 2015).

23. "King's Dream Remains an Elusive Goal; Many Americans See Racial Inequality," *Pew Research Center*, August 22, 2013.

# GLOSSARY

**amnesty**—Official pardon for crimes.

**de facto**—As a result of facts.

**de jure**—As a result of law.

**freedman**—Former slave who is now free.

**Harlem Renaissance**—Cultural and artistic movement in the 1920s and 1930s in which African-American music, literature, and other art forms flourished and became popular with the general public.

**manslaughter**—Crime of killing someone without evidence of malice or intention to kill.

**overseer**—White employee of a slaveholder who was responsible for the work of slaves.

**poll tax**—Fee required of voters in Southern states, used to keep African Americans from voting.

**ratify**—Make something valid by giving official approval.

**servitude**—Slavery or other condition in which one person worked for another.

**slave codes**—Laws in the South before the Civil War that regulated what slaves could do.

**subservient**—Under someone else.

**voucher**—Document issued by a government agency that is used to pay for all or part of a child's schooling.

# FURTHER READING

## BOOKS

Archer, Jules. *They Had a Dream: The Struggles of Four of the Most Influential Leaders of the Civil Rights Movement, from Frederick Douglass to Marcus Garvey to Martin Luther King, Jr. and Malcolm X.* New York: Sky Pony Press, 2016.

Arora, Sabrina G., ed. *The Great Migration and the Harlem Renaissance.* New York: Britannica Educational, 2015.

Berlin, Ira, Marc Favreau, and Steven F. Miller, eds. *Remembering Slavery: African Americans Talk about Their Personal Experiences of Slavery and Emancipation.* New York: New Press, 2007. Originally published 1998.

Jacobson, Sid, and Ernie Colón. *Three-Fifths a Man: A Graphic History of the African American Experience.* New York: Hill & Wang, 2016.

Killcoyne, Hope Lourie, ed. *The Civil Rights Era.* New York: Britannica Educational, 2015.

Learner, Laurence. *The Lynching: The Epic Court Battle That Brought Down the Klan.* New York: William Morrow, 2016.

# WEBSITES

**African-American History**
*afroamhistory.about.com*
A wealth of information about African American history and topics.

**"African-American Odyssey," Library of Congress**
*memory.loc.gov/ammem/aaohtml/exhibit/aointro.html*
The Library of Congress's vast African American collections.

**Civil Rights Movement**
*www.history.com/topics/black-history/civil-rights-movement*
Important information about the Civil Rights Movement, including first-person accounts, videos, and photographs.

# INDEX